Just As It Is In Heaven

JUST AS IT IS IN HEAVEN

For discounted orders or any other inquiries, please contact
jpacilio@yahoo.com *or visit* **jpacilio.wordpress.com**.

Just As It Is In Heaven

An Ordinary Man Encounters the
Supernatural

JOHN PACILIO

Endorsements

I really love and appreciate the ministry of John Pacilio! His balance of biblical truth with the experiential dimension of life in the Spirit is important to me, and John teaches and practices these well.

His faith for healing is contagious, and his teaching significantly raises the level of our expectations. The miraculous results speak for themselves: healings and victories abound!!

I recommend his book and his ministry very highly!!!

Dr. Clayton Ford
National Chair, Holy Spirit Renewal Ministries
Author, *Called to high Adventure*
Pastor, La Jolla Christian Fellowship

"I know John to be a person who practices what he preaches (and writes). He has been coming to our Homeless outreach for quite some time and praying for people and we have seen many people healed, some miraculously. He combines the preaching of the Gospel with healing and faith for the miraculous and the combination of these produces fruit!

John did a healing seminar at our church and several people reported either being healed or impacted significantly by the Lord. The people in our church have been inspired to press into the area of healing because of what he has brought us, so I strongly recommend both his book and his ministry to anyone needing healing or training.

Robert Clement
Senior Pastor, Hope Vineyard Christian Fellowship
Ramona, California

Contents

Introduction

I met Mario at an outreach to the homeless in San Diego. Each week some friends of mine from Hope Vineyard Church go to a local park and bring a hot meal for them. But my purpose for being there was to give these folks more than just a meal. I wanted to give them what I discovered they should have; the love of God, health and healing in their bodies and an encounter with Jesus, the loving Savior and Healer.

Mario looked to be in his late forties; he was bent over with obvious curvature of the spine and was walking with a cane. After introducing myself I asked him what was wrong. He said he had severe problems with his lower back and terrible pain in his back, down his legs, numbness in his feet and toes that curled under. When I asked what the level of pain was on a scale of 1 to 10 he said "11." He said that the doctors had tried many different things to help him but could do no more and wanted to connect a morphine/pain pump to his spine so that he could get relief from the excruciating pain. They had exhausted all their attempts to help him. I could see pain and hopelessness written all over his face.

When I offered to pray for him he eagerly accepted. I placed one hand on his lower back and the other on his stomach and began to pray. He was a short man and in order to do this I had to bend over a bit so I wasn't looking at Mario's face or upper body. After only about a minute or two of prayer I asked him how he was doing and how the pain level in his low back and legs was. Mario said something that I didn't understand.....He said, "I'm straightening." Because I was so concentrated on his lower back and the pain going down his legs I pretty much ignored his words and said again "how is the pain in your back and legs?" He replied, "You don't understand, I'm straightening....my back is straightening!" I looked up and sure enough his back had straightened to the point where I wouldn't have guessed he had curvature of the spine! He said with a mixture of awe and excitement "I'm as straight as you!" There was a look of shock on his face and to be honest, the same look was on mine. I was both confused and delighted. I was excited about his back straightening but confused about it because I was praying for his back and leg pain.

My excitement about his back straightening also raised my level of faith to continue to go for the rest of his healing. I figured if God was straightening his back surely He wanted to heal him completely.

I continued to pray for his back, legs and feet and after just a few more minutes he said, "All the pain is gone and my toes are uncurling!" I was more than thrilled about this but confused about his toes uncurling. Mario said that the problem with his toes was part of the problem with his back. I still didn't quite understand. I asked him to bend over and then to go for a short walk. He did so and came back overjoyed that God had healed him!

I don't think my feet touched the ground all the way home that night! This poor man had suffered for years with a life sapping condition and now he was free!

A few weeks later I had a regularly scheduled checkup with my doctor and after telling her about Mario's healing she said with some disdain, "Well, that would be a miracle." I smiled to myself because many people have the same reaction to the miraculous and then I asked her about the toes uncurling. She said, "Some people's toes curl under because of severe back pain." Now I understood.

If I had to condense what took place with Mario and his overwhelming problems, I would have to say that for Mario at that moment in time at the homeless outreach, the will of God was done for him as it is in Heaven. Simply stated, Jesus said to pray ".... Thy Kingdom come, Thy will be done, on earth as it is in Heaven." If Mario were in Heaven where the will of God rules, his back would be straight, the pain in his back and legs would be gone and his toes would not be curled under.

If someone asks the question "Why did this happen?" My answer at this point in my adventure with a supernatural God is this:

The loving heart of God had Mario's healing in it before we prayed and the loving will of God was that Mario would be healed at some point. What took place that night was a simple intersection of the heart and will of God as it is in Heaven, Mario, and my prayers and declarations offered in faith for him.

The purpose of this book is to share with you my adventures in the realm of bringing more of the will of God as it is in Heaven to earth so that more hurting, broken people can experience the here and now love **and power** of Jesus.

Perhaps through you!

After all, Jesus said: "**Anyone** who believes in Me, the works that I do shall He do...." I just happened to be an "anyone" who was willing to believe that God cares about people, wants them well and would use an ordinary nobody like me.
How about you? Do you believe in a God that loves people to the extent that He would do something like this? Is it conceivable that He might just want to use you as He used me? Did Jesus really mean **anyone** who believes?
The "Mission Impossible" TV show and movie had this catch phrase: "Your mission, if you choose to accept it." So, I say the same to all who read this book. This *can be* your mission also if you *choose* to accept it!
So, let's go on one *very* ordinary man's journey into the supernatural of a God who wants earth to be much more like Heaven.

Forward

There is always more to God than we have experienced. To many folks this is a no-brainer statement: "Yeah, of course there's always more to God, duh!" But others, me in particular, can sometimes settle into a place of believing that we have pretty much figured God out in most of the important areas. We can get our theology, doctrines and traditional teachings together in a neat package and move into that comfortable place of "knowing God."

And yet, very often God wants to show us there is so much more to Him than we have concluded or figured out. When we hear of things about God and what He might be doing in other places and with other people, we can too easily discount the reports because they don't fit in with our neat package. The result is that we may be limiting God and what He really desires to do and therefore miss out on some extraordinary aspects of His nature.

This book is my story of discovering much more of God in the area of "as it is in Heaven," "the Kingdom of God," healing and the miraculous. Over the past ten years I have discovered there is way more to God than I have ever thought or imagined. The best part of my journey is that God is not finished showing me how much more there is.

I wish I could say I have discovered all there is to God and His desires in these areas but I can't. In fact since my entrance into this realm in 2000, I feel as if I have barely placed my toes in the great ocean of the "more of God."

Have I seen more healings and miracles in recent years than I ever have in my 30 plus years of being a follower of Jesus? Yes, hundreds!

Am I thrilled about what I have seen and experienced? Yes! Am I overjoyed that some people no longer have sickness, pain or debilitating oppression in their lives? Absolutely! Am I satisfied or content with the number of people healed or freed by the power of God? No! Do I believe God is satisfied or content with the amount of healing power being released through me or others in His church? No!

But, because I simply believe that He has so much more, I continue to try to find out how much more there is!

Some key Bible verses for this book are the words of Jesus in:

John 10:10: The thief (satan) comes to steal, kill and destroy. I have come that they may have **life** and have it more **abundantly**.

John 14:12: I tell you the truth, **anyone** who believes in Me, the works that I do shall He do.....

Luke 8:10: ...to you it has been given to **know** the mysteries of the Kingdom of God...

Luke 11:2: ... Thy Kingdom **come,** Thy will **be done** on earth as it is in Heaven...

Matt 10:7-8: And as you go, preach, saying, "The Kingdom of Heaven **is at hand,** heal the sick, cleanse the lepers, raise the dead, cast out demons..." (Emphasis mine)

The overall premise for this book is this: there is an entire planet that is hungering and waiting to experience Jesus. And, because every person on the face of the earth is created in the image of God, in their spiritual DNA there is an inbred hunger for Him. But what they deserve to experience is the same Jesus who walked this earth 2000 years ago and a Jesus who is doing today *exactly* what He did then.

But, if we present a Jesus to them who is not the same as He was 2000 years ago, a Jesus who does not heal the sick, diseased and injured today, does not heal the broken hearted today, does not set free the spiritually and emotionally oppressed and those who are captive to the demonic and their own sinful lusts, how can we possibly wonder or whine about why people don't flock to Him as they did 2000 years ago?

My experiences, as described in this book, have proven to me what is written in the book of Hebrews chapter 13 verse 8; "Jesus Christ, **the same** yesterday, today and forever." I hope you will come to the same conclusion.

1

"Lost"
My personal reality show

In order to give you the best picture of why I am writing this book and what it has to offer you I have to go all the way back to the summer of 1978.

For me it was a hot and miserable summer in New York. Hot, because of the very humid summer weather in the east, but the misery was not from the heat, it was from a gnawing, deep emptiness and desperation way down in my gut. Something was very, very wrong, but for the life of me I could not figure it out.

You see, at age 36, I should have been a pretty happy and contented guy. I had the things that some people my age would envy. I was married to a wonderful, beautiful woman for 12 years, had a delightful eight-year-old son, a small house in suburban Long Island, a few bucks in the bank, friends and family and even a slightly used Eldorado in the driveway. (New Yorkers tend to drive Cadillacs you know, at least New York Italians do). I was earning a decent salary co-managing my family's restaurant and my future should have looked pretty good.

Having been born in Brooklyn and raised in an Italian-American family I had taken on the culture of the macho New York/Italian guy, right down to the pinky ring and gold chain and horn around my neck and the outward bravado. Being the youngest of three boys in my family I was spoiled when I was young and used to having my own way as I got older.

But since graduating college, getting married, serving as an Army officer in the mid-60s, and opening and selling two businesses, emptiness became my constant companion and only got deeper and deeper. I found myself trying to fill that emptiness with alcohol, marijuana, gambling, partying and other unmentionable diversions. (Hey, this was the groovy, far out lifestyle of the 60s and 70s, right?)

I had bought into the idea that the things I was doing could help soothe the pain and longing in my heart. I went after them with gusto only to find that after many years of trying to fill the void I only felt more empty and miserable. Although I knew the things I was doing were wrong and unfulfilling I didn't know where else to turn. I was simply grasping onto the stuff that the world around me offered, just like most people I knew. I actually believed my friends and family knew what they were doing, so I followed their lead. I didn't realize they were as lost and searching for answers as I was.

In my ignorance and naivety I was also hanging around with two small-time Mafia wise guy wannabe's, Donnie and Joey, and even thinking that they had a lifestyle to be envied. They didn't work; they drank, gambled a lot, partied and always had a fat wad of $100 bills in their pockets. The spiral down the crapper of my life almost resulted in me leaving my wife and running with these guys! My brain must have been made out of Mozzarella, how dumb could I be? But I didn't think I was dumb at the time.

My typical day would end with me closing up our family restaurant and looking for some fun at a local watering hole or after hour's club. (These places stayed open till 5 or 6 AM.) I always looked forward to a few blasts of scotch at the end of the day to "unwind."

But, what was really unwinding was my marriage. To the utter desperation of my poor wife Fran I would regularly stay out very late and sometimes all night. I would get loaded and drive drunk or high many nights of the week. God only knows why I didn't get myself killed.

Yeah, I tried hard to straighten up many times, but to no avail, I just couldn't cut loose of the lifestyle. I thought that maybe I was going, or arrived at, crazy.

I continued to search for some semblance of fulfillment and answers but none came. The emptiness, the darkness, and my desperation increased.

Although I was born and raised up in the Catholic Church I didn't find many answers there either, but to be honest I wasn't really looking to the church or God for anything. Nah, in my rebellion, that God stuff was for losers. Please believe me when I say I have the highest respect for the people of the Catholic Church and feel a heart kinship with them to this day. But, I never did "get" church. For most of my youth it was in Latin and I just didn't understand what good going there did. The priest would say some things that I didn't understand, tell the people to sit, then stand, then kneel. I would follow along without knowing why. There would be smells of incense and then smoke and then bells would ring and I would get confused. When I did attend, which was seldom, I would go along with the crowd, doing what they did till it was over.

I know the priests meant well and were really trying to serve God and the people *but I didn't get it*. Actually, it was a bit scary because I often felt that God was out to get me. "God will punish you" is a phrase I had heard often in my home every time I did anything wrong. I heard about it in church also. Who needed that!

I would see the crucifix and Jesus hanging on it and kind of feel sad and scared but it never really sunk in what it meant. Although I went to the required Catholic pre-communion and pre-confirmation classes when I was about 11 or 12, all I did was basically learn enough to do what was required to pass the classes and fulfill my obligation. Any semblance of a personal, caring, loving relationship with Jesus either was not communicated to me or I was not listening. I guess I was just trying to get through this stuff in order to do what my parents wanted me to do. So, in my mid-30s God was not someone I was looking for. I figured I had been there and done that God thing in my youth. I tried but it didn't take. Not to any extent of really knowing God. I had **never** heard that God wanted to know me personally and that I could know Him the same way.

Again, let me say I have deep respect and love for Catholic people and I am not against them at all or in any way. I am simple trying to help you understand the emotional confusion *I was in* at the time. In fact I would love to renew my ties to Catholic people and become a loving friend to them.

A "far out" encounter

At age 36, in the depths of my self destruction and desperation a friend of mine whom I had not seen in several years came back into my life.

George and I were casual friends in the 60s and early 70's. We would occasionally party together drinking and smoking dope. Now, a close mutual friend said, "George is back in town and we should get together with him, except for the fact that he has become a 'Jesus freak.'"

Whoa, hold on now! You see, my wife's brother had become one of those "Jesus freaks" about five years earlier and tried to convert us. But I was having none of it and every time I saw him I would run the other way. He was kind of scary, having a full beard, shoulder length hair and carrying a huge and ominous black Bible under his arm! Yikes! No thanks!

So, my friend's statement had me a bit confused and very wary, but he said one more thing that really grabbed me. He said, "But George really seems to have peace in his life and his marriage is together." This touched me because I had sub-zero peace in my life and my marriage was going down like the Titanic. But, the idea that a guy I used to know, who used to do all the stuff I was currently doing, had his life and marriage **together** was extremely appealing.

So I called George and said something like "I don't know about this Jesus stuff, but I'd really like to find out about you and your life."

George came by one night while I was working at my family's restaurant and we went to a corner booth to talk. I remember bringing him to the most hidden booth in the restaurant just in case he had a Bible with him or talked too loud about "you know who." I certainly didn't want any of my friends to see me talking about "religion."

As we talked, I started to get real with him for some reason. It may have been the first time in my life that I uncovered some of what was really going on inside of me. I didn't tell all of course because I didn't want to look like a wimp (I think we used the term "square" in those days). I had to keep up with the happy face.

I was to discover later that this is the face that many people put on so that others won't really know what's going on inside. I was a pretty skilled con-man and putting on this face and being a New York macho man was pretty easy. But I did reveal to him that I was searching for some answers to the emptiness of my life and hadn't found any.

I don't remember much of what George said that night but I do remember being attracted to his peaceful demeanor. He was different than the guy I used to party with. He seemed to care about me and what I was saying. He said he would like to talk more with me and Fran and he invited us to dinner at his house. After George left I started to feel just a little bit of hope that maybe he somehow had an answer. I don't know what it was, but just talking to him kind of lifted me a little. I began looking forward to our dinner together.

About a week later George and his wife Maria welcomed us to their home. The talk over dinner was mostly chitchat and catching up. I was relieved that I didn't hear about any of the "Jesus stuff." They said "grace" before dinner but it was ok because even people on TV did that. But after dinner, George brought the subject up, asking if I was still interested in talking about how he and Maria had found peace.

Peace? How they found peace? If only they knew how much I longed for peace.

As Fran and I sunk into their living room sofa, George proceeded to pull out a big black Bible. Yikes! There it was! Another scary looking Bible! But, I really wanted to hear what changed in George's life, so I took a big gulp and decided to listen. He proceeded to tell us how their lives were changed by Jesus and started to go through the Scriptures explaining who God was and how Jesus was the answer to all my questions and all my searching. He shared about how their lives were spiraling out of control just like mine and how Jesus put them and their marriage back together.

He must've gone on for what seemed like an hour talking about people in the Bible I had never heard of except for Jesus and Moses. I remembered Moses from the movie with Charlton Heston. I honestly was getting a bit anxious and impatient with George. Why was he taking so long to get to the point? I was here to get some answers! Inside I was saying, "George, I came here to find out what to do to fill the emptiness and all you're doing is talking to me about people in the Bible." I was really getting frustrated, I wanted the answer and I wanted it now!

What came out of my mouth was something like this, "George, all that is fine, but I really need to know something important, what did you **do** that caused a change and what do I need to **do**?" He seemed real happy about this statement and said, "John, what you've been looking for all your life is Jesus. That huge hole inside of you can only be filled by Him. I tried to do it with all the things you've tried. What you need to do is get down on your knees, ask Jesus to forgive your sins and invite Him to take over your life."

In the next and longest 10 seconds of my life a zillion thoughts went through my mind. "What? Who me? Get on my knees? Is that it? Don't I have to get my act together? It can't be as simple as that! On my knees!? Head for the exit!

But, all my mental objections seemed not to matter. It felt like this was something I really needed to do. Believe it or not, this strong, tough 36 year old macho man found himself sliding off the couch onto his knees. My mind was saying "what the____ are you doing!?" Yet another part of me was saying "this is right, this is a good thing." Before I knew it I was praying a prayer along with George asking Jesus to forgive my sins, come into my life, take over and fill the emptiness. I chose to repeat the prayer word for word believing that something would actually happen if I did. It only took about a minute and then it was over.

George and Maria again seemed to be very happy because of what I did but I was saying to myself "Is that it?" The evening was over but I was wondering if anything at all had happened. Before we left, George said he would call me the next day so we could get together and talk some more. For some reason I was open to this, but I didn't know why. I also felt just a little different and didn't know why either.

I went home thinking about everything that was said and done at George's house and wondering what it all meant. Did I really get on my knees in front of everybody? I felt a small change in me, a shift of sorts, but I had no way to describe it. It was like a tiny bubble was forming in me and was starting to rise to the top. I really don't remember much more about that evening except I went to bed.

Yikes! Me, Born again?

I woke up knowing that something was very different!

We all know the cliché statement "This is the first day of the rest of your life." Well, when I woke up I knew that this **was** a new day and that I **was** a different person. Don't ask me how I knew, I just knew. I woke up feeling free and clean for the first time in my life. That little bubble that started the night before began to grow in me. It was now a bubble of excitement and hope. Mostly hope. There was hope in me now that things could be different, that the searching, emptiness and longing might be over, that the future could be better and that I finally might have found the beginning of meaningful peace and purpose. I was actually... could I really say it...just starting to feel happy about my life and my future!

I discovered later that it was not just **what** had happened to me but **Who**. It was a Someone and not just a something and that Someone was Jesus!

Could it be? Could this Jesus be real? Did He really care about me... even love me? Did He really die for me and my sins so that I could experience Him, and life to the full? Have I really been forgiven of **all** the crap I had ever done? All of it? It seemed too incredibly good to be true. I was to find out that it was incredibly good and true.

My appetite to learn more became huge. I had to know more. I may have finally found the answer and I had to know if it would last.

George and his wife Maria were very excited about the decision I had made. I honestly didn't know why but I later found out that without my knowledge they were praying for me for about five years and my acceptance of Jesus was the answer to their prayers. Over the next couple of weeks they intentionally made time to spend with me and talk about my future. They told me more about Jesus. They began to explain Scriptures which started to make some sense about what had happened to me in their living room. Those Scriptures began to make total sense and became crystal clear. I didn't know it but they would become foundational truths that would sustain me for the rest of my life.

To my amazement, I found that my need for drugs, alcohol, partying and many of my other nasty behaviors was simply gone! I wasn't even thinking about those things anymore. It seemed like the grip they had on my life had been broken. **Something** much bigger, much more important, much stronger and much more gratifying and exciting had taken their place. **Someone**, rather!

It wasn't about a distant God or going church anymore. It wasn't about being perfect or sinless or even good enough. Jesus came into my life just as I was and started an inner transformation. I didn't have to try hard to be good or a better person, it was just beginning to happen. Change began, but it didn't happen all at once. Jesus, I was finding out, was a loving, caring and most of all very patient Savior and friend. He was taking His time with me. Even today His patience, with me and my faults, weaknesses, mistakes and sins, is incredible.

But my wife Fran did not have the same experience I had. She was skeptical and hesitant about all that was said and done. She was especially skeptical about me because of my history with her. I had led her on a pretty miserable roller coaster ride for the previous 12 years. I was a crazy man and I did crazy things and I hurt her badly. This Jesus stuff could be just a phase that I would soon get over. So she took a "watch and wait" approach to all that was unfolding. She needed to personally know that this Jesus we were all talking about could keep me on track and could be personally real for her.

So during those couple of weeks when George and Maria were talking with me, she came along and listened. And at one point Fran, who had suffered depression for several years, asked Jesus a very personal question. She said, "Jesus, if you are real you can take away this depression." Within days, to her delight, Jesus answered her prayer, the depression was gone and she invited Him into her life also! In the course of about two weeks our eight-year-old son Chris also came to the Lord. So here we were, a new family, together, and embarking on an amazing journey together.

Jesus had become very real to us. He wasn't just someone who lived 2000 years ago. He wasn't just the person who was talked about in the Sunday school classes of our youth. He wasn't church, He wasn't ministers or priests, He wasn't just that figure on the crucifix. He had become life to us in the here and now and a promise of a good future. He would be with us here and in the life to come. He healed our lives; put our family back together and became the very substance that held us. He wasn't distant, He was here. He was real, He was all we would need for the rest of our lives, He was...everything!

We were discovering the reality of the words Jesus spoke in John 14:6 "I am the **Way**, the **Truth** and the **Life**." Nothing would ever be the same again.

Three decades later these words of Jesus sum up the deep meaning of what Jesus came to do for us and everyone. It's about **life**! But not the life many people experience, no, it's about **the life** that only comes from God the Creator of life. And it's not a thing but a person, Jesus. In the previous Scripture Jesus says, "I am.... **the life**." In other Scriptures Jesus says, "... I have come that you might have **life** and **life to the full** (in abundance)." "He who believes in the Son (Jesus) has **everlasting life**; but he who does not believe in the Son **shall not see life...**" "the Son gives life..." and "I am the Bread of Life." John, one of the 12 apostles, says, "**He who has the Son has life, who does not have the Son does not have life.**"

We can all have the kind of life that the world and people and things can give us. The question is "how is that working for you?" I tried that kind of life but I found that it did not satisfy. And, anyone reading this book cannot have a satisfying fulfilling life without Jesus Christ. I'm sorry if it sounds dogmatic or non-inclusive, it's simply the truth according to the most truthful man who ever lived!

But, by having Jesus, by receiving and knowing Him, the **God kind of life happens.** The Bible says that not only does Jesus **have** life, **He is life** and when we have Him we have true and lasting and powerful and eternal **life**. And, with the **Jesus life** with us and in us, **everything** falls into place.

The wonderful God kind of life happened to me and my family because we let Jesus happen to us.

By the way, you may be wondering what happened to my two hoodlum friends. After I came to Jesus, I went to both of them and told them what happened to me. I suggested that they strongly consider what I had done and think about doing the same thing. I told them that God could turn their lives around also, but they were having none of it. They pretty much brushed me off with disdain. I remember both of them saying that I would wise up and be back with them soon.

The tragedy of their rejection of Jesus was that Donnie was arrested for racketeering and was sentenced to 25 years in prison without the possibility of parole. I kept in contact with him and found out that he did all 25 years! I also heard that my other friend Joey was arrested and had been sentenced to 15 years. I have cried for both of them. I wonder how many nights they cried themselves to sleep, perhaps wishing they would have listened to me and turned over their lives to Jesus Christ.

The wonderful part of this story is that God saved me from a similar fate. Given the direction my life was going I very well could have been hurt, jailed or killed.

Unfortunately, like me, many people believe they are in control of their destinies.

They simply refuse to let anyone, including God, influence or direct their future. I am so glad I did.

While my friends were doing time in jail God began rebuilding my marriage and orchestrating my future.

But my friends decided that Jesus was not relevant to them and decided to take a place of neutrality about Him. ***Neutrality about Jesus is not an option.*** A person cannot say "Oh, I believe that Jesus existed and that's good enough." Or "I'm not against Jesus." No, Jesus said, "If you are not **for** Me **you are against** Me!" Being for Jesus means just that, being for Him, His words, His ways, His desires and living it out the best we can. Lip service will not cut it. Only a heart acceptance and belief in Him gives a person the life that Jesus has for them and gives eternity in Heaven.

The development of my "Good News"

My excitement about the new life I had discovered increased and in the months ahead I became like a person who had the experience of seeing Star Wars, Rocky and Avatar all rolled into one. I had to tell everyone! I just had to talk about my newfound freedom, my joy and my experience of discovering this new life in Jesus. It just kept bubbling up from the inside. I looked around me and what I saw was people who didn't know what I had or what they could have. I saw people in search of meaning and happiness all around me and I knew I had the answer. I had really good news to share. If Jesus could change my life for the better He would of course change theirs…if they only knew.

So I began to tell pretty much anyone who was warm and breathing about Jesus and my experience! The result of my exuberance was that I made a lot of people really glad or really mad. Many people that I spoke with eagerly accepted Jesus and a new life with joy. Many others thought that I had become some kind of cultish, religious nut, one of those "Jesus freaks."

The word was out, "Johnny has found religion and he's out to convert you, watch out!" In my early days of sharing my experiences I know at times I came across as dogmatic and heavy-handed and I apologize to all the people whom I offended because of my over the top attitude and insensitivity. But to be honest in looking back, I can't and won't apologize for the Truth that I shared with people about Jesus. It was true 2000 years ago and it remains true today. It was true for me in 1978 and it remains true for me and all today.

Although I was hurt by the rejection of some of my friends and family I continued on telling my story. What developed and stayed with me over the next 30 years was a deep personal relationship with Jesus that no one could sway me from. It was just too wonderful! Many tried to "snap me out of it," no one succeeded. What happened back then will remain the best thing that ever happened to me in my entire life! And my attitude was and is "I don't care who doesn't like me because of Jesus." I wouldn't trade the last 30 years for anything, especially to get approval from people. What a waste it would be to trade Jesus for people's opinions!

What developed over the next 20 years is what I will call "my gospel/my good news." Since gospel means good news, I wanted this good news to reach as many people as possible. This good news is what I shared with hundreds and hundreds of people during that period of time. It was simply this: "Jesus is real and He loves you, He died on a cross to pay for your sins, He wants to take away the emptiness and longing you have deep inside, He wants to be invited into your life, He is what you have been looking for all your life and when you ask Him He will give you forgiveness of sins, eternal life, a new life and a new relationship with Him." This was the essence of my good news and I shared it as "the good news" from then until the year 2000 when "my good news" enlarged dramatically and became more like "the good news of the Kingdom" which Jesus and His disciples preached. Why the change? What's the difference?

I was about to find out and walk into the realm of God's version of good news. It would include the supernatural and the miraculous and it would change me forever.

2

A longing fulfilled

Since the time in George's living room in the summer of 1978 a new person emerged. I wasn't just changed I was radically changed. I wasn't just different I was radically different. I became one of those people I used to joke about, a "Jesus freak." My life had been so transformed that I could not stop talking about it. If you were around me for any length of time you would hear about Jesus and my story. It was natural and it naturally flowed out of me.

What had happened to me without my even knowing about it was that I became what is called "born again." This is also called "born from above" or "born of the Spirit." There is no other way to explain it. It was as if a brand new me was emerging.

I was to discover that what I was experiencing was talked about by Jesus. And what I shared with people revolved mainly around a few Scriptures in the book of John Chapter 3. In verse 3 Jesus says: "…. unless one is born again (from above, of the Spirit) he cannot see the kingdom of God."

That was it! That's what happened! I was born again and I had a peek into the Kingdom of God, a peek into the realm of a here and now Savior and King! I was able to begin to see God's plan and purposes for me. A Heavenly reality was forming around me. Things began to be clearer and it was wonderful! And I realized others could have the same wonderful experience **if they wanted to.**

The rest of what I shared with people was from the same chapter where Jesus gives the reason why this "new birth" happened to me and how it is available to all. In verse 16 Jesus says:

...for God **so loved** the world (every person) that He gave His only son (Jesus), so that **whoever believes in Him** shall not perish but shall have eternal life. For God **did not** send His son into the world to **condemn** the world, but that the world (every person) through Him might be **saved** (rescued and made whole). (emphasis mine)

"**So loved,**" did you hear it? I was "**so** loved" that Jesus would take the punishment I deserve for my sins! He chose to take the brutal beating, scorn, shame and humiliation for me! He chose to take the pain of that crucifixion so that my sins could be paid for. Someone had to pay in order for me to be right with God. It was either going to be me suffering in eternity to pay for my sins or Jesus payment made on the cross. But, because of this great love He chose to do it for me and for you

God **so** loved me that He did it for me. Me, dirt bag John, was loved, no, **so** loved! Something I had been looking for all my life was to be **so loved....this loved!** Freely given and unconditional, this love, acceptance and forgiveness was mine!

The reality of this would sink deeper and deeper into my heart as the days went on. Wow!

This would become the experience I would refer to as I talked to people over the next 20 years. It would form the basis of what I will call "my good news."

The offer of this gift of forgiveness of sins and eternal life and a new and fresh start was **free** to anyone who would believe in Jesus and I offered it to many freely. I was honestly very disappointed and sad when people simply rejected this offer. It has often brought me to tears, because to my heartbreak I also discovered that the rejection of Jesus and this gift would result in separation from God for eternity.

Jesus clearly outlines this in the next verse of that passage. He goes on to speak about Himself when He says in verse 18: "Whoever believes in Him (Jesus) is not condemned..."

That was me. I simply believed in what Jesus did for me by going to the cross and personally turned over my life to Him. It was wonderful news, but there was bad news to follow in this passage. Jesus goes on to say:

But he **who does not believe is condemned** already because he has not believed in the name of the only begotten Son of God (Jesus). And this is the condemnation, that the light (Jesus) has come into the world, but men (people) loved darkness rather than light because their deeds were evil. For every one practicing evil hates the light and does not come to the light, unless his deeds should be exposed. (emphasis mine)

The "Message" bible says it this way:

This is how much God loved the world: He gave His Son, His one and only Son. And this is why: so that no one need be destroyed; by believing in Him anyone can have a whole and lasting life. (Heaven, too) God didn't go to all the trouble of sending His Son merely to point an accusing finger, telling the world how bad it was. He came to help, to put the world right again. Anyone who trusts in Him is acquitted; **anyone who refuses to trust Him has long since been under the death sentence without knowing it (destination Hell). And why? Because of that's person's failure to believe in the one and only Son of God when introduced to Him.**

This is the crisis we are in: God-light streamed into the world, but men and women everywhere ran for the darkness. They went for the darkness because they were not really interested in pleasing God. Everyone who practices doing evil is addicted to denial and illusion and hates God-light and won't come near it, fearing a painful exposure.

In the next few months I must have read these Scriptures 100 times realizing that God had done an amazing thing for us all.

To put these Scriptures in my own words, I see that God offers us a wonderful free gift of love and rescue and life. In essence He's saying:

Look what I will do for you because I love you so much. I will take care of the sin problem that separates you from Me. I will send my Son to pay for your sins so that you do not have to pay for them yourself. Although your sins deserve punishment, I will place the punishment on my Son Jesus. And, when you believe and trust that He has done this for you, then you will have life beginning at that moment and continuing on throughout eternity. But, if you refuse what I offer you, you will be responsible for your decision and the consequences of it.

The consequences include not only separation from God in this life but separation after death and for eternity in hell.

God mercifully and continually extends this gracious offer of the free gift of forgiveness of sins and eternal life to all on an ongoing basis. **But the choice to receive the gift remains ours.**

It's as if two people are in the ocean 500 miles from shore when their boat capsizes. A rescuer in a boat comes by and offers to save them. One of them is glad and says yes and is saved from drowning. The other refuses the help and decides that he can make it to shore on his own.

In one Scripture Jesus talks about some who were not willing, He says "but you are **not willing** to come to Me that you may **have life.**" John 5:40

That is what is going on every day all around the world. Some are seeing their need and accepting the rescue. And some are simply denying their need of Jesus and are rejecting the offer. The rejection of Jesus results in the fact that payment for sins will be made by spending eternity away from God in Hell.

There are people whom I love dearly and whom I have talked with about these truths, but they have rejected Jesus. Several close relatives of mine have done this. One of them has rejected Jesus since I began to tell him my story 32 years ago. My heart breaks for him. I know that God will give him every opportunity to change his mind right up until the day that he has to give a personal account of his life to God. Another very dear relative actually heard Jesus speaking these words, "come to me" but decided not to respond to His kind invitation.

I will continue to love them and pray for them both. They may have years ahead to change their minds or they may have days but no one knows except God.

But the good news is that Jesus is waiting right now. The offer of Jesus and life is still available. Included in this life is healing both of the body and the soul. Jesus said He came to heal the brokenhearted. This means that all who have been wounded, mistreated or hurt by people can be healed. He also offers healing from oppression. Chronic fear, loneliness, low self-worth, anxiety, depression, psychological disorders and addictions of all kinds can all be healed through Him.

Even now as you read this book, if you don't know this wonderful, loving Jesus; this life, this hope, this peace and love can be yours in a heartbeat. You are a whispered prayer away from real life. Will you ask Him? Will you simply express your need and desire for Him and for true life? He has been waiting for you all your life to simply say "Jesus, help me; forgive me of my sins and save me from the emptiness of this world around me." "Come please Jesus and give me life." "I believe that You died on the cross to pay for my sins so that I don't have to pay for them." "Come into my life and heart." "I

receive You, I receive Life." If you ask Him, I promise He will give you what you prayed for.

What next? Tell someone. Anyone will do. You probably have a Christian friend or relative who would like to hear about this. Get a New Testament and begin reading and find out about Jesus and the new life you have begun. Start hanging out with other followers of Jesus.

I sincerely promise, you will not be disappointed by this decision!

Continuing to tell my story

Over the next three decades I would tell hundreds and hundreds of people. And because of my personal story and my sharing of these Scriptures, hundreds would receive this free gift and have similar experiences as I had. Some declined politely and some declined not so politely, as in "get lost." But I went forward.

Healed by simple faith in a promise from the Bible

In 1981 my family moved to San Diego, California. But what went with me were un-diagnosable stomach problems. These began soon after I made a decision to be a follower of Jesus. Many doctors tried to help, but, increasing pain, discomfort and resulting depression followed. I became very confused and disillusioned. I knew Jesus was the best thing that ever happened to me but I had all kinds of questions about why I was sick. I would read in the Bible how Jesus healed everyone who came to Him. Yet, I would ask Him to heal me and ask others to pray for me without any results. Because of the debilitating symptoms of my illness I began to long for Heaven. Depression increased and desperation deepened.

I decided that I would do whatever was necessary on my part to be healed. This included a deliberate decision to forgive anyone who had ever hurt me in any way. I discovered that I was harboring bitterness, resentment and anger towards people who had mistreated me in the past. I asked God to show me who I needed to forgive and I did so from my heart. In some cases I wrote letters asking for forgiveness for things I had done to them. Although this was not easy, I was finding out it was essential to leading a healthy and peaceful life.

The stomach problems continued for 10 years. But, one day, in 1988, I was in my bedroom reading the Gospel of Mark. In Chapter 11 Jesus comes upon a fig tree in leaf but without any fruit on it. He commands the fig tree to die and later when the disciples see the tree again it is dead. When they asked Jesus about it He proceeded to give them a lesson on praying with faith.

In verse 22 Jesus said to them "Have faith in God. For I assure you, whoever says to this mountain, 'Be removed and be cast into the sea' and does not doubt in his heart, but believes that those things he says will be done, he will have whatever he says."

To me He was saying "See what happened to the fig tree, the same can happen to your sickness if you do what I'm telling you."

And then the following words of Jesus really went deeply into my heart: "Therefore I say to you, whatever things you ask when you pray, believe that you receive them, and you will have them."

Although I had read these Scriptures before, this time they affected me. I decided that I was going to take Jesus at His Word, believe that I had received healing for my stomach, and act accordingly. I remember writing down my decision and coming out of my bedroom to show it to Fran and a friend who was visiting. In fact I was so determined to prove that Jesus words were true that I asked them to sign the paper and date it. They did.

From that moment on I made the decision to believe I was healed and I started to act on that belief by doing the things I could not do before, things that would cause discomfort. Over the course of the next three months I was challenged on a daily basis to believe. Sometimes it was pretty scary. I would open the refrigerator and decide to eat foods that before had caused discomfort. When asked how I was doing I would reply that I had prayed and believed I was healed. Slowly the symptoms diminished. In 2 to 3 months they were gone completely! In the days, weeks and months since then, symptoms have tried to return but I would have none of it, rejecting them. I knew what belonged to me now and I was determined to keep it. I remain symptom free to this day!

Without knowing it I had another glimpse into God's will being done as it is in Heaven. Let's look at the facts. For 10 years I had been immobilized by stomach pain and discomfort. When I discovered God's will for me as shown in the Scriptures outlined above and when I decided to believe and act upon His will, my healing began. It was as if this gift was mine all the time, described to me by Jesus in the Scriptures, and all I had to do was believe and receive it. The problem for me and perhaps for others is that there is a lot that belongs to us but because we are not aware of it or because of our tradition of unbelief, we do not get the benefit of it.

Discovering what really belongs to us

Learning this became a foundational part of my life and therefore I'll expand on it.

I heard a story that may help illustrate what I'm talking about. I forget who originally told the story, and perhaps no one knows, but it's a good one. It's about a poor immigrant family who saved diligently for many years and purchased tickets to sail from Europe to America. They bought the cheapest tickets and brought along enough food to sustain them on the journey.

They shared this meager food among themselves and stretched it so it would last. But on the last day of the journey they decided to celebrate their arrival in America by buying a dinner for themselves in the ships dining room. As they entered the dining hall they showed the steward their tickets and asked how much the dinner was. "Oh," he said, "this dinner won't cost you anything since it's already included in the price of your tickets."

The Bible states that, "...My people perish for lack of knowledge." You see, healing was the will of God and was already provided for Mario, the man I told you about in the introduction. It was also provided for me. But, both of us never knew it. When I brought these truths to Mario that he could be healed, when we believed and we acted on it, he was healed. When I discovered in the word of God that I could be healed, believed and acted on it, I also was healed. These healings were in the heart and will of our Father in Heaven and all we did basically was believe that God wanted His will done "on earth as it is in Heaven." They were revealed to us and we simply received what was already there. (The price of the tickets included meals.)

Now some people have gone to an extreme to believe they can "name and claim" anything. This is foolishness and can lead to disaster. But **when God reveals to us individually** a truth about what can be ours or what belongs to us, we can appropriate it for ourselves. I am not trying to develop a method or a formula here. What I am saying is that sometimes God has much more for us than we have discovered. I want to encourage you to discover for yourself more of the blessings or benefits of being a child of God.

It was about 1988 when I discovered this but it would be another 12 years before "the Kingdom of God and the Will of God as it is in Heaven" really began to sink in and become a strong force in my life and ministry. In the meantime I was to answer God's call on my life.

3

"Declare My Kingdom, and I will come…"

su·per·nat·u·ral
1: of or relating to an order of existence beyond the visible observable universe; especially of or relating to God or a god, demigod, spirit.
2 a: departing from what is usual or normal especially so as to appear to transcend the laws of nature b: attributed to an invisible agent.

Around the time of my stomach healing I began doing volunteer work with an organization called Youth for Christ. Billy Graham helped form this organization in the early 50s. Part of their outreach to youth in San Diego was a program called "Youth Guidance." This was an outreach to "at-risk youth," some of whom were incarcerated in San Diego's juvenile jails.

Commonly called Juvenile Hall or "Juvie," at any one time there were over 400 kids from the ages of 11 to 18 locked up there. They were in there for offenses that ranged from truancy and pot smoking to murder, rape and arson. Some of them would go on to spend as much as 25 years to life behind bars.

My thinking in those days was that if God can transform a jerk like me who was heading for disaster, he could certainly transform their lives also. So I volunteered and began organizing and leading a weekly Bible study/chapel service in one of 14 units in juvenile hall. The youth assigned to these units were divided up by age, gender and severity of their offenses.

Over the next two years, we spent time with hundreds of confused, hurting, lonely and spiritually lost boys and girls. I would always gear our meetings towards the goal of these kids coming into a personal relationship with the loving Savior. I felt that this would be the best thing I could do to empower them to lead a different and more productive life. In our meetings 30 to 40 kids would attend and usually several would pray the same prayer I prayed back in 1978. They would pray in a response to my presentation of the same "good news" which I responded to and which transformed my life. To say the least, I was delighted with this ministry.

Faith is spelled R-I-S-K

During 1989-1990 the volunteer ministry was thriving but I was becoming more and more dissatisfied with the business I owned and began seeking God about the reasons for my dissatisfaction. I felt Him indicate strongly that His grace was not on my business and that He wanted me to make myself available for His business on a full-time basis. There came a point where I felt God saying that I should give away my business and become "His minister."

This would be a major and radical step in our lives. Although it was really good news for me it was also very scary. Was God actually speaking to me? Did I really hear correctly? Give away my business? What would I do? I wasn't a pastor of a church or even on staff. There was no one asking me to leave my job so that I could come to work as a minister with a salary.

When I went to my wife Fran with this she didn't really see it as good news at all. In fact she was pretty scared and thought I was a little bit crazy. After a few weeks of discussion we agreed that I would do as I felt God was showing me but if financial provision didn't come within a reasonable period of time I would conclude that I did not hear God correctly and get back to work.

I felt God was leading me to give my business away to a friend of mine who had a similar business. I did so and about two or three days later the director of the Youth Guidance Ministry at San Diego Youth for Christ called me and asked if I would be interested in her position. She was going to be leaving in a few months and just happened to think of me when she was considering who would take her place! This seemed to be the confirmation that I was looking for. Here was a door that only God could have opened and I decided to go through it. That was the good news part.

The bad news part came when I met with the San Diego director of Youth for Christ who informed me that they would love to have me join their program but that there was no salary funds available. Gulp! Here I was once again at a crossroads. A full-time ministry job but no financial support.

But God had graced me with a sense of knowing that this indeed was a door opened by Him and I concluded that if it was, provision would follow. I took the risk and accepted the job.

Jesus provides

I was hired on in September of 1990 and went to work overseeing the Juvenile Hall ministry which consisted of about 3 weekly chapel programs with about a dozen volunteers involved. I did a series of fundraisers and support started to come in.

During this time a member of the board of directors of San Diego Youth for Christ decided to donate $1000 per month for one year to my ministry! This was something that only God could orchestrate! By December funds were coming in that were equal to the amount of money I was formerly making in my own business!

I felt like Peter who got out of the boat wondering whether the water would hold him up. What Peter and I didn't know was that the Lord would hold us both up if we just kept our eyes on Him and not on the dangerous and scary circumstances around us.

Over the next eight years God blessed this ministry to the extent that we expanded every year. The Juvenile Hall administration gave us great favor and allowed us to bring a chapel service or Bible study into all 14 units of juvenile hall. I trained and placed over 80 volunteers into the system. The result was that we went from ministering to about 50 -60 kids a week when I first started in 1990 to ministering to about 300 a week by 1994.

God gave us favor at every turn. At one point, a man came to my office saying that he was sent by an anonymous benefactor who had heard about our program and wanted to donate to our ministry. This man donated $49,000 so that we could start a mentor match program for kids who were being released from juvenile detention!

Things seemed to be going so well, but I was unaware of some underlying forces at work that were leading to a crisis.

Health problems again

Along around 1994 I started to have mild headaches in the late afternoons. These got worse and worse and doctors couldn't help. By 1998 I was unable to continue and had to go on disability and give up the ministry as I knew it. I didn't know it but the headaches were to plague me for the next 12 years. I had unfortunately forgotten the promise of God that I had discovered in dealing with the stomach problems. And to be honest my focus during my years at Youth for Christ was on the ministry and not on the Lord. When I tried to come back to a place of faith for healing I was unable to get the results that I got before. But because God is a faithful redeemer He led me to an even greater experience of His love and power in spite of these circumstances.

In 1998, although I was on disability because I was unable to maintain an 8 to 5 work week and although I still had headaches, I couldn't sit still. You see, the calling continued to be a force in my life.

A friend of mine introduced me to a woman in Tijuana, Mexico who had a ministry to the poor indigenous natives. These were the people who could be compared to our Native Americans. These people were in Mexico before the Spanish overtook the land and began persecuting them and they are still persecuted to this day.

When I met this lady and saw the needs of the people she was ministering to, my heart went out to them and I began to help as best I could. I would go down to Tijuana, the border only being about 20 minutes from my house, and I began to minister alongside this lady. We brought food, clothing and built shelters. Of course during our time with these people we shared the love of Jesus with them, many of them coming to the Lord. I basically preached the gospel (my good news). This was that people could find forgiveness of sins, eternal life and a personal relationship with the Lord Jesus. I was to find out that God wanted to change my gospel to His gospel, the Gospel of the Kingdom.

A wonderful new adventure begins

In 2000 I began to get a desire to do evangelistic outreach in a broader sense. I started to plan to do a weekend evangelistic campaign in the vacant lot on this lady's property. We built a platform, wired in some lights and started to pray and prepare for a three day weekend outreach. We would be handing out flyers inviting folks to come for a free meal and to hear "my good news."

But during the months prior to doing this campaign there was a hunger developing in me to see some of the same things that accompanied the gospel in the early church. These were the healings and signs which we all get excited about when we read the gospel accounts of Matthew, Mark, Luke and John.

I had been to some meetings by a man named Randy Clark. In his meetings one could see a clear display of power as people would be healed of pain and sickness and set free from demonic bondage. I was seeing and hearing about first century signs and wonders and miracles happening today. I knew this was something that I **had to** not only experience for myself but share and offer to others.

The healings and miracles and testimonies were valid and obvious. I remember at one of the meetings Randy saying that anointing and power for these things can be imparted or transferred from one person to another. He talked about the history of the church from the time of the book of Acts to today bearing witness to these things. He shared how Jesus imparted to the disciples and how the disciples continued the impartation down through the ages.

Believing that this was the case and was what I needed, I went forward for prayer and the laying on of hands for this impartation. I remember Randy saying the impartation takes place whether you feel anything or not. Randy laid his hands on my head and spoke some words about healing, signs and miracles but I didn't feel a thing.

During my prayer time in preparation for the Tijuana evangelistic campaign I began to simply ask God how could I be used to bring healing and the miraculous to the hurting and lost. I specifically wanted to see these things happen at the upcoming campaign.

During one of my prayer times I felt the Lord's quiet but strong voice speak inside of me saying "Declare my Kingdom and I will come." That's all He said. I really didn't know what this meant so I had to continue to seek Him for more of the fullness of this word. And what I gleaned from the times of seeking Him was that if I would declare that His kingdom is here and now and that His power, rulership and dominion over the works of the devil is here and now, then God would demonstrate His presence and power. People would be healed just like with Randy Clark.

I felt I was to apply this to the meetings that were about to take place. And I felt that I was to apply this just as Randy Clark had done in his meetings. It was a bit scary because Randy used to declare that the Kingdom of God was at hand and that people would be healed even without anyone personally laying hands on them. And I saw this take place in several of his meetings. Randy used to say something like "While I am preaching the power of God is going to come on some of you and you will be healed or much improved. So, while I am preaching, those of you who came with pain and your pain has decreased significantly or completely, please raise your hand and wave at me so that I can acknowledge what God is doing."

Then Randy would pray from the platform. Sure enough as he preached a message people would start to wave their hands and Randy would acknowledge them and simply say "Thank You Lord for what You are doing."

For some reason I felt a strong assurance that God would do the same at our upcoming weekend outreach.

So the day arrived. The Friday night meeting was all set. The flyers were handed out, people started to arrive and the musicians began to play. Only about the 40 or 50 people came out the first night and they were made up of Mexican people from many walks of life. There were some homeless, some well off, some curiosity seekers and onlookers and some believers. As I went up on the platform I couldn't believe how confident I was feeling about what God was going to do.

Confidence - turns to fear - turns to joy

I greeted the people through my interpreter and began to tell them how much Jesus loved them and how He wanted to personally interact and show them His love that night.

Then I said it. I told them something that I thought I would never say in my lifetime. I said: "because Jesus is the same yesterday, today and forever and because the Kingdom of God is here and now and because His power, rulership and dominion is present, several people will experience that in a very real and tangible way. I'm not only here to talk about someone who lived 2000 years ago and did some really great things back then. I'm here to preach about a here and now Jesus who is doing the same things today! Jesus Christ who healed **all** who came to Him 2000 years ago is the same and He still rules today over sickness, pain, disease and demonic oppression. If what I am saying is true about Jesus you will see people healed or experience healing yourself."

In my quiet times before the Lord I had already dealt with the voices that were telling me that I was not worthy to do this, holy enough to do this, prayed up enough, fasted enough etc. The devil threw at me every reason why I should not do it. And of course he accused me of testing the Lord and being presumptive. I had to pray through most of the crap that he was telling me. I think the reason why I was confident when I walked up on the platform the first night was that I had dealt with these lies already. And I was in a place of simple faith that if God can use a person like Randy Clark He could use me. I had come to a place of understanding that if I was to see more of God in my ministry and be able to preach about a here and now Jesus who was the same yesterday, today and forever, then I was supposed to go through this weekend in faith that He had my back.

The statements I made on that Friday night were all based on the character and will of God that I had seen displayed in the life and words and works of Jesus. The heart desire of God to heal and deliver and set free hurting humanity was to be displayed. Although I was confident, while I was actually doing the preaching I felt my knees shaking a bit, but I was determined to continue.

I asked for a show of hands of people who had come to the meeting in pain. About eight or nine people raised their hands. I told them that I was going to preach a message and that while I was preaching God was going to take the pain away from some of them.

I started preaching about the Kingdom of God and how Jesus had brought it and demonstrated it by healings and miracles. I went on to talk about this Jesus being the same and doing the same things right now. About 10 minutes into the message I asked the crucial question, "How many of you who came in pain are no longer in pain and all your pain is gone?" It seems that God would not let me say "some of your pain is gone or you are experiencing a little relief." No, he wanted me to ask if all the pain was gone.

I waited. No one raised their hands!

Gulp! The confidence that I had when I first walked up onto the platform was quickly draining out of my feet. But, for some reason, I felt that I should not back down from my original statements about people being **completely** free of pain. And now I was faced with a dilemma. I knew what God had told me to do and yet the results were not there. I took another deep gulp and decided to continue preaching. During the next few minutes of preaching about the Kingdom my mind was racing with all kinds of thoughts about why I had not heard God, was this presumption and how I had gotten myself into this jam. I can't remember but I probably was wondering if they used tar and feathers in Mexico!

I finally decided to try one more time, but I was really ready to give up if nothing happened. So I said again, "alright, of those who raised their hands before indicating that you came in pain, how many of you are free of pain?" About 10 of the longest seconds I have ever experienced went by and then I saw one hand being raised and then another...no two or three and then another! A total of about four or five people had raised their hands indicating that they came in pain and all their pain was gone!

It was hard for me to believe even though I had preached it. Maybe they hadn't heard the interpretation correctly, so I made sure the interpreter told these people exactly what I was asking. I made sure these people knew that I was addressing only people who had come in pain and **all** their pain was gone. I didn't want to take a chance that they had misunderstood what I was saying. The interpreter restated what I had asked **and the hands stayed in the air!**

Faith and joy returned to me! Wow! Woweee! Wow! Although I didn't let a lot of people see it, I was dancing inside! God was amazing! God could do anything! And I was thinking that He might just do even more that night and in the next two days.

I invited those people to come up on the platform and simply give their account of what happened to them.

You need to understand something. These poor Mexican people are pretty humble folks and they don't volunteer to be in the spotlight let alone be on a stage and talk into a microphone to a crowd of strangers. So, I was surprised when about four of them came up and through the interpreter I learned that long-term and short-term pain in shoulders, necks and backs was completely gone! These very poor people who might not even be able to afford a doctor or treatment encountered the love of God! **This Jesus who might have been far off previously was now very close to them!**

I wish I could remember exactly what they said, but I can't. I guess I was still in a state of awe and wasn't hearing clearly. My mind was racing with thoughts of "Oh my God, this is incredible, what do I do next, what does God want to do next."

But I do remember that there was a sense of elation that spread into the crowd like a wind. Joy, awe and faith was at hand and rising! The Kingdom had come and the King had brought His power and authority as it is in Heaven with Him!

What impacted me the most was that for the first time in 20 years of being a follower of Jesus Christ I was able to point to four healed people and say "What has happened to these people is the evidence that Jesus is alive and cares about people. It is a demonstration that the words that I'm saying to you about Jesus are true." I was able to say for the first time in my life "if you don't believe the words that I have been speaking to you, believe what has happened to these people!"

I talked for a few more minutes about Jesus and how He loved them, wanted to come into people's lives, forgive their sins, give them eternal life and begin a relationship with them. I then led those who wanted to make a decision for Jesus in a prayer. I discovered there wasn't a whole lot of persuasion necessary for people to come to faith in Jesus. The healings that these people saw spoke louder than what I was saying to them. A bunch of people made decisions for Jesus!

I then asked some friends who had come with me to come up front to be available to pray for more people who had physical or emotional needs. I asked all who were sick, injured or in pain to come forward for prayer promising that God was not done yet. Several more people reported being healed or freed of demonic oppression that night.

There was a sense of well-being and joy as the night closed and we were privileged to give these folks food and clothing. Everyone was smiling. These people got more of what I now call "The Kingdom of God Gospel." They were offered not only eternal life and forgiveness of sins, but healing, freedom from oppression, hope, food, clothing and an opportunity to have a life transforming encounter with Jesus in the here and now.

To use a bad pun, they got the whole Enchilada.

I went across the border that night happy and content but knowing that things in my future were going to very different. Different in an amazingly good way!

Two more meetings were held that weekend and God showed up and did even more than He did on the first night. One of the most amazing things that took place was that a pastor's wife got healed. She was listening from her car because she was in too much pain to walk to the seating area. Her back got healed simply by her listening to what was being said! No one prayed for her or laid hands on her! I was to joyously learn in the months and years ahead that God was not limited by our traditional beliefs of how He does things.

Let's take a moment and think of what actually took place over those three days. The Scriptures say that Jesus only did what He saw His father doing.

In my opinion just about every time Jesus looked, His father was healing the sick, freeing the demonized, raising the dead and preaching the good news that He, the King, had brought His Kingdom with Him. When Jesus looked to see what the Father was doing He saw the Kingdom and the will of God being done on earth. Jesus demonstrated what He meant by praying and teaching His followers to pray "...Your Kingdom come, Your will be done on earth as it is in Heaven."

On that weekend in Tijuana the will of God as it is in Heaven was demonstrated on the earth, on that patch of dirt in Mexico. The will of God as it is in Heaven was that people who came in pain would go home free of pain; people who were demonized would leave free; sick people would be made well and they would experience a little bit more of what it is like in Heaven. All I did on that weekend was tap into the will of God as it is in Heaven and take the risk of declaring that God wanted it done on earth then and there!

Some might say well, were all the people who were sick healed, were all who were oppressed freed? What about you John and your headaches? The answer is, probably all the sick were not healed and my headaches were not healed. I don't have the full skinny on why not, but in the chapters ahead were going to be talking more about these things. One thing for very certain is that the Kingdom of God was declared and people got healed, and had an encounter or saw someone have an encounter with God.

You would think that after this experience in Tijuana I would have run out and bought the tent and hit the road to do "healing services" all over the world. Well, it didn't work that way. Over the next three years my adventure into the supernatural of God looked more like a roller coaster ride than a bullet train.

I couldn't have been happier about what took place that weekend but, I had to go home and still deal with questions and personal life problems.

4

"…the thief comes to steal, kill and destroy…"

Over this period of time I continued to pray for people for healing with slowly increasing improvement of results. My enthusiasm waned after the Tijuana experience. The main reason for this was my own struggle with sickness. The headaches simply would not let up. I struggled in a kind of a tug-of-war with God about why I wasn't healed.

Believe me when I say I tried everything I knew to be healed. I went everywhere and had every "anointed" healer type person lay hands on me. All the doctors could do was prescribe more pain drugs. Those drugs came with their own set of problems. Unfortunately "my healing" became the overwhelming focus and a dominant force in my life.

I managed to continue following the call on my life, tending to my family, serving in church, praying for others and leading a home group. During this time I also immersed myself in books and teachings by people who had experiential insight into healing and the miraculous. What I mean by experiential insight is this: we may hear teachings about Jesus and His healings and miracles. We may hear teachings about God wanting to do these things today. And all this is valid and true. But when it comes from a person who has actually proved these things out in their own lives it means so much more.

Bill Johnson was one person who was easy to read and listen to. His down to earth manner was very appealing and the results he and his church were seeing were amazing. He reminded me so much of John Wimber, one of my heroes and whose books had impacted me in the 90's. Bill is the Pastor of Bethel Church in Redding, California. In the

90s, after an encounter with God, he determined to make healings and miracles a normal part of Christian life for him and for his church. This fell so much in line with my desires that I devoured his stuff.

I also read several books by other prominent leaders and pioneers in the faith. My diet began to become one of feeding on the Gospels and what these leaders said **and did**. I read books by Smith Wigglesworth, William Branham, Maria Woodworth Etter, Amy Semple McPherson and contemporary leaders like John Wimber and Randy Clark. **All these people and many more have developed a 1st century church lifestyle and value system that would not accept a powerless gospel.** Their determination to make a supernatural lifestyle more natural was what I was after. And I truly believed it was what God wanted me to be after.

More risky business

In 2003, I decided to go to Veracruz, Mexico. The man who interpreted for me in the Tijuana outreach was the pastor of a tiny church about an hour outside of this city. He had asked me several times after the Tijuana meetings if I would come to Veracruz and do an outreach in his town. I had put it off over and over again simply because of my struggle with pain and my lack of energy. But now I felt I had to come to a decision. Would I continue to let the fact that I was not healed deter me from moving forward in the Kingdom, in the will of God and the call on my life? I decided to accept his offer to come to his town.

With the help of a friend we put together some funds to buy food for this very poor Mexican church. We sent the funds down to the pastor and made arrangements to go. Our budget could only afford for me to go and while I was still dealing with my fears and reservations I boarded the plane to Veracruz. All the way there I had to deal with the fact that I was still not healed of chronic headaches. I wish I could say it was easy.

Also, in the days before I left for Veracruz I started getting fearful thoughts about how demonic a place it probably was. I knew about the witchcraft, occultism and superstition that was rampant in this region of Mexico. To be honest I was getting a bit scared of going. But when I asked the Lord about this He seemed to say "Are the demons in Veracruz worse than the demons in San Diego?" The obvious answer was no. This relieved some of my concerns.

When I got off the plane on that Wednesday night I ran into a searing wall of heat and humidity. It was so oppressive that I wanted to get on the next plane and go home. The thoughts that were running through my mind were about how I was going to deal with this heat and the headache pain. I was really struggling.

What I hadn't really learned yet was that my enemy, the lying accuser, was at work in my mind trying to give me all the reasons why I shouldn't be doing this type of ministry and especially going deep into a remote region of Mexico. These were the thoughts he was throwing at me and that I was buying into... "How can you be preaching healing when you are still sick, isn't that hypocrisy?"... "This heat, coupled with your pain is going to be too much for you to handle."... "Not much is going to happen here."... "If you eat any food here you're going to get very sick." "The people here are not going to accept a gringo." "The demonic attack here will be very severe."

After about an hour's ride on a bone jarring pot holed road we arrived at the small, very rural village of Cuya Cuenda, a dirt road town of perhaps 200 people. We went into a small church where about 35 people were waiting. It was very obvious that this was a "dirt poor village" and these were very poor and humble people. I would learn later that most of the men who could find work earned the equivalent of about $8 to $10 a day. Some of the families lived in one room dirt floored houses made of sticks. And yes, even some believers lived like this.

And yet these people had come to a meeting on a Wednesday night after a long hard hot day and they dressed in their Sunday best. And although I could see hardship and weariness on some of their faces I also saw hope and faith and a hunger for God. I didn't know it then but these people were "the blessed poor in spirit" that Jesus referred to. They were to see and experience God in the days ahead.

Pressing through

Although I was not "feeling it" and was somewhat miffed at the oppressive heat and other conditions it seemed like as soon as I walked into the church and was introduced by the pastor something changed in me. As I started to speak to the people an excitement and joy started to build in me just as it had Tijuana. I would come to learn that this was what is called an "anointing." It's a tangible feeling of God's presence and excitement.

The people there were very happy to have me come and minister to them. They had been told by the pastor of the things that took place in Tijuana when he was interpreting for me. It may well have been that they were more confident of seeing the power of God than I was.

The welcome I received was more than warm, and I started to relax as I thanked them for inviting me to come to their village. I started to go into the story of what took place in Tijuana, the pastor interpreting for me once again just as he did there. I tried to be as honest with them as I knew how and when I was finished telling them about Tijuana I did what the Lord instructed me to do three years earlier. I told them that the Kingdom of God was here and now and that God alone rules over all things and especially their problems, sicknesses and all the works of darkness in their lives. I declared to them what I declared to the people in Tijuana that God would show himself to be powerful and take away pain and sickness from them.

I asked how many people were in pain and three or four people raise their hands. I preached a few minutes and declared the sovereign rule of God over pain, sickness and disease. I broke the power of oppression and the assignments of darkness. I released to them the love and power of Jesus and asked if anyone was free of pain. Only one person raised a hand and told how they had come in pain and now all their pain was gone. I can't remember the exact nature of the pain, but this was different, only one person. I knew there were more sick and in pain there but how did God want to touch them?

I then felt led to tell them that God wanted to use anyone there to heal the sick and set people free of oppression. I spoke for a couple of minutes about how Jesus said "anyone who believes in Me the works that I do shall he do...." I told them that I loved this Scripture because it was so inclusive. It disqualified no one and included everyone who believes. I shared what I had learned from Randy Clark. Randy loves to say "God can use little old me." I went on to say that if God does not disqualify us from being used then we should not disqualify ourselves for any reason.

You see, I had proved this out over the last three years. God had used me in Tijuana and around San Diego and although in my own sight I was not holy enough and I did not pray or fast enough God still used me. I was well aware of my shortcomings... I got angry too often... I spent too much time in front of the TV... I certainly didn't read the Bible enough...etc. but I have discovered something in the years following this, that all believers including myself are pre-qualified to be used by God.

Why? How? Because our qualification came through Jesus' fully completed and finished work at the cross. I found out that in the sight of God I am completely holy and I am in right standing because of Jesus. How much more righteous can one be than having the righteousness of God? I have had to learn to put my weaknesses, mistakes, sins and faults in their proper place as I go to minister to hurting people. The proper place for all those things is under the Blood, remembered no more and in the sea of forgetfulness.

Bill Johnson likes to say, "I cannot afford to have a thought in my mind that is not in God's mind." This highly respected pastor, whose books have been read by thousands, talks a lot about our true identity and the fact that God has promised to be with us. If Jesus said I will never leave you then when are we alone or without His power? Bill Johnson says:

> God's covenant promise, "I will be with you," has always been linked to mankind's need for courage to face the impossible. There

is no question that the presence of God is what brings us great comfort and peace. But the presence of God was always promised to His chosen ones to give them assurance in the face of less than favorable circumstances. The great commission provides more interesting reading for those who remember what kind of men God was giving his charge to...greedy, prideful, angry, and self-centered men. Yet Jesus called these to change the world. What was the one word of assurance that He gave them before departing from sight? "I will be with you always...." (Matthew 28: 19).

So I told this group of God hungry believers that God was ready and willing to use whoever was ready and willing to be used. I asked for those who had come with sickness disease pain or oppressions to come up and make a line to my left. About eight came up. I then asked those who wanted to be used by God to heal the sick to come up. About six came up.

I then did a quick prayer model for them. I prayed for someone who had an injury and was in pain. I did this to demonstrate how easy it was to pray for people. This person had a shoulder injury and it was difficult for him to raise his arm. I found out that he had injured it in an accident and proceeded to pray the simplest prayer I could. I think I basically said "shoulder be healed and pain leave now in the name of Jesus."

After praying for him I turned to tell the people what I had done and why. While I was talking the man I had prayed for began to move his arm and shoulder. He was behind me as I was sharing. I shared about how Jesus prayed simple prayers of power and authority and how He didn't spend any time asking His father to heal or set a person free. I told them how Jesus only did what He saw His father doing and that just about every time He looked His Father was healing the sick, raising the dead or driving out demons. I went on to share a little bit about the power and authority that they had resident in and with them because of what Jesus did. And I told them that when they prayed for others it didn't have to be begging God to do something that He already wanted to do. It was to be a prayer of confidence that God wanted that person healed and well and therefore it could come out in the form of a command.

When I turned around the man I had prayed for had a big smile on his face and was moving his arm and shoulder around, God had healed him.

I then did what Randy Clark did in one of the meetings I attended before Tijuana. I told the people who wanted to be used by God that the pastor and I would lay hands on them and pray an impartation to them.

For me this is simply transference of anointing and an affirmation that God can and will use them.

I matched up the pray-ers with the pray-ees and told them to pray just as I had. In just a couple of minutes, as I was casually talking to the pastor, everything got quiet. I asked the pastor why they had stopped praying and he went over to the people praying and inquired. He came back to me and said "they're done." I said "what do you mean." He said "everyone is healed!" Mighty man of faith that I am, I couldn't believe this and I sent him back to double check. He reported back to me the same thing "everyone is healed."

In my own mind I was battling with thoughts of unbelief and doubt. Everyone who came for prayer was healed? This couldn't be. I've never heard of anything like this before! It really didn't sink in until much later that I had heard about this happening before in the Gospels, when everyone who came to Jesus was healed. But at that time and moment I could not put the two together. This was by far the most mind blowing event that happened in my ministry to that point. I asked the pastor if some of the people could give their testimony.

Then several of them gave their own personal reports of how God had healed them and taken away their pain. Pain of all kinds was described but my mind was so reeling from this that it is difficult for me to remember the reports exactly.

But I do remember one man in particular and as I'm writing this story tears come to my eyes because of his need and the joy that followed. He was a man who had a wife and five children and they lived in one of those one-room dirt floor stick houses I described to you. He had suffered for a long time with pain in his knee. He struggled every day as he went out to work in the fields to provide for his family. Yet he would go because he had to go. And I could sense that although this man had a lot to complain about he was not a complainer and that he and his family loved the Lord. He told, through tears, how all the pain in his knee was gone and how happy he was to be able to go to work without any pain.

I told everyone that we would gather together the following day, put packages of food together, go door to door in the village giving out the food and praying for the sick.

The most absurd thing took place after this meeting. Most people would say, "Wow, John, you must have been flying high and been so pumped, you must have felt wonderful." But, as soon as I left and went back to my room, the joy and elation that I felt began to be clouded by unbelief about what really took place, the oppressive heat, and the pain in my own body that still was there. I was to learn that I didn't have the tools in place to handle this battle in my mind and also it would have been good to have a close friend to talk to and pray with. I would have to fight this battle over the next four days and even after I returned to San Diego.

Hindsight helps

But now in looking back on that night in that small seemingly unimportant church I can see from a different perspective. What we would call a supernatural event took place. And from our perspective it was a supernatural event. **But from God's perspective it was a very natural event**. Natural, because in God's Kingdom in Heaven there is no sickness or pain or disease. In the heart and will of God, health and healing was already provided for these people. Once again an intersection of circumstances took place. God's will once again was done in this poor village church just as it is in Heaven. All the ingredients for miracles were in place; God's will, the hurting people, and someone who would take the risk of declaring that God wanted them well.

So, what does the will of God look like? It looks like whatever Jesus did and said when He brought Heaven to earth. It happened that way to a large extent that night in Veracruz.

Can it be as simple as that? Yes. It can be if we start to see things from God's perspective (healing being His will and nothing impossible) and not from our own perspective. As I said before Jesus only did what He saw his Father doing and every time He looked His Father was healing, delivering, freeing, helping, and blessing. Jesus simply did the same.

I believe doing what the Father is doing is both specific and general. Specifically we could say that Jesus saw His Father spit on mud and put it into the eyes of the blind man so he could see. But, generally it is the will of God that blind people see. Specifically, we could say that Jesus saw His Father command the cripple man to rise and walk, but generally it was the will of His Father that cripples walk.

And yet in the story of the Centurion we find Jesus getting up to go and lay hands on the Centurion's servant. We would assume that that is what He saw His Father doing. But when the Centurion said that all Jesus had to do was say the word, Jesus in essence said, "If you believe that is the way it can happen, you got it." So, can we conclude that the will of God was to heal the Centurion's servant but the exact method was according to Jesus and the Centurion's faith? God's ways of healing are not fixed or rigid, as in this case of the Centurion's servant.

For me it is fair to conclude that the will of God according to the life, words and works of Jesus, is that today all who come to Jesus, (even through His followers) should be healed. The in–our-faces fact is that Jesus healed all who came to Him and that will of God as demonstrated by Jesus as He instituted the New Covenant has not changed. Why? Because Jesus has not changed. His is the standard to be reached for!

The New Covenant

I am going to try to make some sense about something that is not easy to understand. We find that Jesus demonstrated the new covenant (arrangement/agreement) by healing and undoing the curse of not keeping the law of the old covenant (arrangement/agreement).

Under the old covenant, if someone broke the law of God, He could allow sickness and disease to come. This was part of the "curse of the law." But, the really good news is that Jesus changed things. In Galatians 3:13 Paul writes, "Christ has redeemed us from the curse of the law having become a curse for us." The punishment for not perfectly keeping the law was borne by Jesus at the cross. Therefore, we who come into faith in Jesus are redeemed from this curse He bought us out of.

He actually became a curse for us and was punished in our place. So, the question remains, how much punishment was left over to be put on us? None! If sickness and disease was a punishment under the old covenant and Jesus took our punishment on Himself then there is no longer the punishment of sickness and disease for us!

Under the old covenant adultery meant stoning and when you touched a leper you were made unclean...Jesus reversed this didn't He? A much better covenant is here!

God gets no glory from our sickness or disease (except when we are healed!). He takes no pleasure in harming us, and He never will.

The next day in Veracruz

We should not try to develop formulas. But we can put some basic ingredients together that will help us to personally move forward in this area. God is good and the devil is bad. God gives good gifts and does good things, the devil does bad things. Jesus came to bring life, health and freedom, the enemy comes to steal kill and destroy. Basically, God wants people well and whole. In Veracruz on that Wednesday evening that's what happened.

The next day some of the members of the church gathered together to put packages of food together. I shared briefly with them the principle of giving away what they had received the night before. Jesus, when sending His disciples out to heal the sick, raise the dead, cast out demons and declare the Kingdom of God, told them "freely you have received freely give." Peter in his encounter with a crippled man said to him, "What I have I give to you." The principle is that whatever we receive we are to give away. Then we come back to God, get more and give that away also. Some people call it being filled to spill. I briefly went over the simplest ways of praying for people and combined that with the packages of food that we were preparing and encouraged them in going door-to-door with the love and power of Jesus.

We set out and because I don't speak Spanish very well the pastor and I paired up. At the end of the day we had given food and prayed for many people in the village inviting them to come to meetings to be held on Friday, Saturday and Sunday. There were not any reports that day of anyone being miraculously healed. In fact the pastor and I prayed for a lady with a paralyzed hand and arm. The hand was curled up like a claw and was frozen in position. We prayed for her and asked her if she felt anything and if she could try to move her hand. Nothing apparently had taken place as far as we could see. We invited her to the meetings and left.

The next day she came looking for the pastor and excitedly showed him some movement in her hand. If I was to put a percentage on it I would estimate that she had perhaps an improvement of about 30%. Although I was happy about this I wanted much more for her. But, she was thrilled. As the weekend went on she would receive more and more freedom in her hand.

OMG a circus tent!

Some friends of the church who ran a circus donated a tent to us so that we could have our meetings in an open field. As the first of three meetings on Friday night approached I was still struggling in my mind and my body. I was nervous, I was hot and I had to fight to remember the events that took place in the church on Wednesday night, the lady with a little healing in her hand, and what took place in Tijuana three years earlier. If I had to rely on feelings or the sense of an "anointing" I would have gotten on a plane and headed home, there simply was none of that. This was to be a weekend of moving forward by faith in what God had already done and what He wanted to do.

Perhaps about 80 people showed up for the Friday night meeting and about 100 came for Saturday and Sunday. In the huge tent that was erected they seemed to get lost. I didn't have any fresh insights to share or new "words from the Lord." I simply did what the Lord had instructed me to do in Tijuana. "Declare My Kingdom and I will come." I stuck to that message and God backed it up.

But this time I used the people from the church to pray for others. On Wednesday He had demonstrated His desire to heal and His desire to use ordinary believers to do so. These people not only gave their testimony at every meeting of how God had healed and touched them but also made themselves available to be used by God to touch others.

Over the course of the weekend about 40 more people reported being healed because of the people in this church praying for them! God had accomplished something really great.

God's plan to change the world was being carried out, now by humble, very poor followers who were simply tied into God's will being done **on earth, in their village!** Were they fully trained and discipled in the area of the miraculous, no. They simply believed that God was with them and wanted to heal people through them.

What was really amazing was the fact that God backed up the simple prayers of simple people big-time! How could He not? Was His love and compassion for the hurting people of this village any less because the Christians who were praying were poor or untrained?

With these experiences under their belts these church people would have something powerful to offer. They now had something to give away that didn't cost money to buy. They could say like Peter "I don't have silver or gold but what I have I give to you."

One miracle makes it all worthwhile

As I got on the plane to leave the next day several thoughts were going through my mind. One was of two men who came to all the meetings in wheelchairs and left the same way. Although I had seen or heard reports of 40 or more people healed over those five days, and was thrilled at these results, I could not get these two men out of my mind. But, this disappointment only caused a determination to see people like this healed and it was growing deep inside of me. I would not rest until I saw people more people relieved of their suffering and some get out of wheelchairs.

On the plane I also experienced joy as I remembered praying for a boy who was born deaf and had come to the meetings with his mother. I remember praying for this 18-year-old boy with all my heart and trying to determine if there was any change. I would pray for him and walk behind him and speak some words. I would then come back in front of him and look for signs that he had heard. For a length of time that seemed like forever but which was probably only 15 minutes absolutely nothing happened. There was not even the slightest indication that he was hearing anything. But for some reason I could not give up.

I continued to lay hands on him and pray as I felt led, commanding spirits of deafness to leave, commanding his ears to be open and hearing to return. I did this one more time, walked behind him and said the name Jesus. I came back in front of him and looked in his eyes and they were wider than before. The look on his face was indicating that something had happened. Any sound at all would be brand-new to him and the look of confusion on his face said that he was beginning to hear. I nodded my head up and down and he nodded his head up and down indicating that he had begun to hear a very little bit! I made a gesture with my thumb and forefinger trying to indicate the amount of hearing he was experiencing. The gap between my fingers was quite small but it was there.

I continued this several times until when I said the name Jesus from behind him, he tried to form the name Jesus with his mouth! It came out quite garbled. I quickly realized that having never heard before he of course had no idea of how to talk. But I recognized his efforts to say the name Jesus! His mother at this point was in tears!

As I sunk down in my seat on the airplane the entire trip, the difficulties, the heat, my own headache pain and every inconvenience was now all worth it. I realized that if no one else had gotten healed on this trip, the look on the face of this boy and his mother was more than enough for me. As I write this my eyes once again well up with tears.

As I tried to get some sleep on the flight back to San Diego, a very real sense of deep joy welled up inside of me as I remembered this boy. It was as if I was feeling the pleasure of God.

Yet there was other questions rolling around in my mind. "God, how far do you want to go with this? Do you want to do in San Diego what you have just done in Mexico? How can that happen, what is it going to look like?

You see, I had heard of these things happening in Third World countries but not so much in the United States. So far most of my experience in this area was in Mexico. I was wondering just what God had in mind. I was wondering about my own weaknesses and the pain that I still had in my head." I was both excited and apprehensive about my future.

5

"Getting over my stuff"

As my plane landed in San Diego I decided that I would begin looking for the answers to the questions I had just asked the Lord. I wanted to see just how far God wanted to go with this Kingdom stuff. I was to find out that the answer was "yes" to the question "Do You want to do this in San Diego?"

I still had to deal with several factors which were hindering me going forward to a large extent. My own health was one of them. The biggest hindrance to my life over the previous 10 years was the pervasive and chronic head pain that I had to deal with. A deep gnawing soul and spirit struggle was going on about this. This struggle had led me through times of depression and hopelessness and times when I just wanted to quit any aspects of ministry life. Here I was, going to doctors, taking medications, and dealing with pain on a daily basis, and now seeing people miraculously healed right in front of my eyes. Not only that, I was beginning to tell people that God wanted them well and that sickness and oppression was not part of God's plan for them. And yet no matter how much I prayed, fasted, pleaded and received prayer from dozens of people my pain remained.

The question that every Christian has asked down through time was the one I constantly asked: "why?" And although I cried out and pounded the gates of Heaven no answer came, at least in the way that I was used to. It seemed this answer would come only over time.

One thing that I would discover over the following years was that God did not give me chronic headache pain. I will loosely quote a comment made by my pastor Ed Noble of Journey Community Church in La Mesa, California. I hope I don't mess it up too much but I believe he said, "God will allow things that are against His will to happen in order that His glory and purposes would be achieved." He described the passage where the disciples pointed out a man who was crippled from birth and they asked "did this man or his parents sin that this would happen to him." The reply by Jesus was "neither this man nor his parents sinned but that the glory of God would be revealed." If Jesus would've stopped right there then we would all have the right say God has a greater purpose in sickness. But Jesus didn't stop there, He proceeded to heal him. In my opinion and according to the words of Jesus, there is no benefit to sickness except in the glory that God gets in the healing of it.

My take on this is that the guy got crippled somehow; it could've been an injury, an accident or the result of sickness. It wasn't the punishment for sin because Jesus said that it wasn't. **But the glory of God was not revealed in his sickness, the glory of God was revealed in his healing. His healing became a demonstration of God's will as it is in Heaven coming to the earth.** His healing was a demonstration of the new covenant of grace and mercy. His healing was a demonstration that there was a new deal and a new sheriff in town, Jesus. And when this sheriff was around the bad guys get run out of town and justice happens. Did God allow this, absolutely. But to what end? The miraculous healing was the end. Jesus didn't say that the purpose of this man being crippled was to teach him something, build character in him or draw him closer to God in the sickness. The healing and the miracle was the purpose and the man would testify and give glory to God about this for the rest of his life!

The freedom of not having to understand

I have a category in my theology. I gleaned this category from Pastor Bill Johnson. It's a category I call "I don't know why and I don't understand." It is very difficult for us human beings to say this and accept it. It seems we have a need to try to understand everything and I believe that is a God-given desire. But there are some things about God we are never to understand until we enter His presence for eternity. I am learning to accept the fact that I do not need to understand everything and **yet still believe in the absolute goodness of God at the same time.**

You see, if I seek the Lord about a matter and do not receive understanding from Him about it, this category really helps me. It's where I place the fact that there is an evil, destructive, demonic force in the world that causes babies to die, famines and earthquakes, disease and destruction and misery. I can use this category and leave my need for understanding to eternity. In the meantime I am continually coming to a place of not attributing evil to the Lord and thereby living unoffended at

God. I refuse to say God gives cancer and other diseases to people. For me it comes down to this. God good...devil bad.

Is God a child abuser?

For the Christian believer and follower of Jesus this is especially important. If we believe that God sends something like cancer to his children we are attributing evil to the Lord. I have prayed with scores of people who ask to be healed yet have been taught or have simply bought into the theology that God sends these things on his children to teach them, make them better or more holy or develop their character. I believe many people sabotage their own healing by believing their sickness is a gift from God. The New Testament scriptures talk about a God who **only** gives good gifts to His children. How can we say otherwise?

The question I ask is, "If you believe God has given you this sickness as a gift in order to do something really good in your life why would you ask to be healed or go to doctors? Why would you want to get rid of this really good gift from God and defeat His purpose and will for your life?"

To really take this to an absurd level, why shouldn't we ask God for more sickness so that we can be made really good and develop really good character? I believe that down deep in our hearts we don't believe sickness is from God. But,I think we reason this way to have some answer for why we are sick. I think we are honestly trying in our own way to honor God because we don't have any other answer and haven't been able to get help. In searching for understanding we try to look for a way that God can make good out of very bad situations.

I think some basic logical thinking in this would help. I will use this example and ones like it several times throughout this book because I believe it is so important.

If a father decided to break his son's leg in order to teach him something or build character in him we would all be outraged and agree that he was a child abuser.

We must decide whether our Heavenly Father is a child abuser or not.

If we came home one day and found our house ransacked and many things stolen would we jump to the conclusion that it was our Father or would we immediately think that it was a thief?

Sicknesses like cancer steal joy, life, health and prosperity from us. Cancer is a destroyer. Jesus came that we might have life and life to the full. And more importantly Jesus says that the thief comes only to kill steal and destroy. Who? The thief, not God! But when Jesus comes on the scene He comes with the opposite intent. Jesus came to destroy the works of the devil.

We must believe that God has many other ways to teach us lessons or build character in us. I have yet to see much good come from the cancer that ravages a person's body and leads to a torturous and painful death.

In Exodus God describes Himself to Moses as "compassionate and merciful and long-suffering." That was an old testament, old covenant description by God of Himself. The covenant brought by Jesus 2000 years ago is described as a "better covenant, a covenant of grace and mercy." If God was compassionate and merciful and long-suffering in the old covenant how much more compassionate and merciful is He in this **better** covenant given to us?

Another question of importance that I was hashing out with the Lord was "God, if You really wanted to heal more people and do more miracles, why don't I see more of it around me, in my church, among good and dedicated Christians that I know." I asked that question in the summer of 2003 coming back from Veracruz Mexico and it has taken me until now to more fully come to some understanding.

For many of my 33 years of following Jesus, when a healing or miracle would happen it was the exception rather than the rule. Compare this to Jesus and the early church where healings, signs, wonders and miracles were the rule rather than the exception. When Jesus encountered someone not getting healed or delivered by His disciples He was not pleased. In fact it sounded like He was a bit ticked off that they were not "getting it."

So, why don't we see more healings and miracles? The conclusion I have come to is that the church has been starved of teaching, mentoring and modeling in the area of healing and miracles for so long that there is very little faith or expectation of these things. Our grid, our mindset, and our view of the supernatural simply doesn't allow for an easy acceptance of, or expectation for the miraculous.

Consider this; the church has been trained and mentored in the fact that a person can be saved by faith in the finished work of Jesus. John 3:16 has been taught, preached, practiced and accepted by the church since the days of Martin Luther. Ask any believer if a person can be saved right now if he believes in Christ and they will say absolutely "yes!" Yet ask any believer if a person can be healed right here and now and there will probably be many doubts.

Why? I believe it is because the church has come up with messed up theological and traditional reasons why God doesn't heal. Why? I believe it is because the church had to have reasons why their loved ones got sick and died. To me, many of these reasons simply make God into a broker of pain and suffering to His children and not the compassionate and merciful, grace giving Father and Daddy that He is.

Cessationism is what I'm talking about. It's the theology that God has stopped doing things as He did then, in the first century church. One of the roots of this thinking is this; **because we don't see** these things taking place today, we conclude that God has stopped doing them. Or we conclude that because the Bible is complete God doesn't need to do these things anymore.

How destructively naïve. Imagine the multitudes of hurting people who have been denied healing because of thinking and teaching like this.

What do you think the church would look like today if along with salvation and justification by faith as taught from the days of Martin Luther, healing, health and wholeness as a benefit of the cross and new covenant was taught also? I believe the church would be much happier, healthier and much more naturally supernatural.

The absolute in-our-faces fact of Scripture is that Jesus healed **all** who came to Him. No one can find any place in the New Testament where Jesus said even once "Sorry, you can't be healed." So, my question is, has the will of God as demonstrated by Jesus changed? If He only did what His father was doing, then the will of God at that time was that all who came to Jesus would be healed. I believe it is supposed to be the same today, because Jesus is "the same yesterday and today and forever." I think the bottom-line is this; the problem is more likely on our end than on His.

God turns the tables

To illustrate what I mean by cessationism and wrong teaching about spiritual gifts, healing and miracles being for today, I'll fast-forward to 2009.

In the fall of 2008 and the spring of 2009 I taught classes on healing at Journey Community Church. There was a man there named Steve and this is his account of what took place. I have included his entire testimony because it is so important.

My Journey to Physical Healing
By Steve Durham

God's healing does not exist in the church today – or so I thought. My name is Steve Durham, and this is my journey to understanding and experiencing God's divine, physical healing.

I was born into and raised in a home where my parents believed in God and took me to church. My childhood included activities like weekly Sunday school, church on Sunday morning AND Sunday night, and of course, mid-week prayer meetings. These could and should not be missed. Extra-curricular activities included church-organized camps, and summer vacation Bible school. In fact, it was at one of these summer events that I realized a choice of eternal consequence needed to be made. When I was 6, I made the choice to confess my sin, accept Jesus as my Lord and to follow Him. I had a protected and wonderful childhood, but I never witnessed a person getting miraculously, physically healed. I knew those around me didn't believe in such things, so I didn't either.

My lack of experiencing God's divine healings as a child was endorsed by academic explanations. When I was 20, my life was going nowhere! And fast. I had no idea of what to study in college as a major. I had lost touch with the living God; despite my upbringing and weekly church attendance. I was empty inside. I had no-one I could relate to that knew and expressed God. So, I was overjoyed when I decided and took my parents suggestion to attend a bible institute in New York – and even more glad they were going to pay! It would be – and was - a place where I could get my feet back on the path to God and really understand "what" and "why" I believe. This bible school is where I learned about "Jehovah Rapha" – the God of Healing. My scholarly Bible teachers, supporting their positions with Biblical and logical arguments and would say things, such as:

"Healing is only for spiritual needs, or Healing is not for physical needs, because such an outward expression would be ostentatious, and the good Christians are humble and meek – not showy." Or, "Physical healing is a fraud, as evidenced by ridiculous television "actors" who are only seeking or trading money from the hopeful and desperate."

I knew those around me didn't believe in such things, so I didn't either..

Well, if early childhood impressions and academic lectures were not enough, the ultra-conservative churches I selected and attended over 4 decades sealed-out nearly any hope of knowing a God who can heal – physically heal. Sure, I prayed for God's intervention thousands of times, and I witnessed the prayers of others. Many of us prayed, knowing in our hearts God can and does save the lost, comfort those in crisis, provide for the needy, and help us pass exams we didn't study for. I witnessed many answers to prayer, and no doubt, protection over my life was an answer to someone's prayer...Mom. Only once in my life did I know of a group of church leaders who performed a "laying on of hands" to a young missionary suffering from a degenerative spinal condition. That young man never did recover completely – yet another nail in the coffin of Divine, physical healing. That was something for Jesus' disciples, but not a gift to be exercised in today's church – or so I thought.

In June 2008, my wife, children and I started attending Journey Community Church. This past fall, I saw an insert in our church bulleting about a special class on healing. I sensed that this was something I should attend. Maybe I would make a friend or two at my new church home. I wasn't expecting anything more than an education or at most knowledge of what Journey Community Church believes about healing. After the first lecture, led by John Pacilio, there was a class exercise to pray for healing over each other. As juvenile as it sounds, I was scared. I had never done this before, and now I am praying for healing...in public?! Perhaps you can imagine my shock. I wasn't quite sure what I had gotten into. It occurred to me that this might be some kind of cult group on the fringes of Christianity. Well, after the exercise, no one in the room was miraculously healed of blindness or deafness. So, I fell back into my comfort zone and attended another class where someone taught on personal and spiritual healing. Now this I could understand and appreciate. By my fourth class, I knew the drill – lecture, then pray. But my life was about to change.

Prior to the class prayer exercise, our teacher, John, asked us to sit quietly, listen to what the Father was saying to us, and then be ready to share whatever we heard, even if it seemed like non-sense. Well, one of the other students sensed there was someone who needed prayer for a shoulder. John asked if anyone in the room had shoulder problems. I sheepishly acknowledged that I had recently injured my shoulder, and was told by my doctor and chiropractor there was little that could be done. So, John had this person who sensed God's speaking pray for me and a few others who had prayer requests. Those in the small group each placed their hands on my shoulder, arm or hand and prayed. There was no healing.

John was making the rounds to each of the small groups, and hearing the outcome of no healing said, "Pray again. This time, I want you to declare and release God's power" and a few other words of encouragement. During the second prayer, my arm started shaking – really shaking. I thought to myself that one of the prayer team members holding my wrist or hand was creating a fake 'Ouija board' experience. When the prayer ended, the group asked me why I was shaking my hand, and I had to be honest – I wasn't intentionally.

Now this was very strange, and not all that different from what I saw on those fraudulent, mid-night television shows. John came over and asked me to check if my shoulder still hurt. I moved my arm like a football quarterback loosening up. No pain. Wait. This is fantastic! No, unbelievable! It seemed surreal, but it was really God teaching and showing – as only He can show – that divine healing can and does occur. Praise the Lord!

I am so glad that my Father in Heaven
Tells of His love in His book He has given
Wonderful works in the Bible, I see
But this is the dearest, that Jesus loves me….
I am so glad that Jesus loves me!

My name is Steve Durham, and my Journey to knowing, growing and showing God's divine healing is only beginning. My prayer is that you too can witness God's healing. Thank you.

I have run into Steve several times over the 2 year period since he was healed and he usually lifts his arm above his head showing that his shoulder is still healed. Before this event Steve had been taught and trained well and had a neat little theology about healing. Poor Steve had suffered like so many others…needlessly. Now he had an encounter with the healer and he can **never** go back to that old worn-out God diminishing theology. It sounded like Steve was actually somewhat satisfied with his old theology. But now it sounds like he is thrilled and overjoyed that Jesus is a here and now healer and loves him! Read this footnote by Steve:

My God, in His forgiveness, prevents souls from entering hell's destruction – even mine.

My God, in His compassion, rescues spirits from despair – even mine.

And my God, in His power, has physically healed me – even me. Jehovah Rapha has an entirely new meaning to me."

One of the most rewarding things to me is the look of awe, joy and wonder on the faces of those dear children of God, like Steve, who get relieved of pain and suffering. I've seen many but I have such a hunger to see many more.

About our inheritance

To me, what happened to Steve was mainly about the inheritance from God that was his but that he was ignorant of. You see, Steve's healing of his shoulder was part of his rightful inheritance as a born again child of God. In the will and testament of Jesus, the New Testament, healing was already provided for Steve. He just didn't know it or appropriated it. God didn't just think of a healing for Chris on that day in our healing class and decide that it was time for him to be healed. No, it was provided for him 2000 years ago.

What if a relative of yours passed away and wrote a will including you in it? Let's say he left you lots of money. You could read that will every day for years and not get the benefit of the money unless you decided it was yours and went to the executor of the estate to collect it.

Some believers read the New Testament and do the same thing. They will read about Jesus healing all the people who came to him, but not appropriate healing for themselves with expectant prayer.

I have already written about the many reasons why people don't know what belongs to them. I urge you to rethink what you have been taught and some of the conclusions you have come to regarding your inheritance. What if there's so much more available that you have not appropriate for yourself and for your loved ones?

So, after my return from Veracruz in 2003, God said "YES" to the question, "Do you want to do this in San Diego?" The adventure was to continue soon.

You may want to pause right here to ponder and pray. You may want to ask yourself:

Am I willing to rethink my preconceived beliefs about God's willingness to save, heal and do the miraculous in the here and now? Am I willing to allow God to change not only my point of view but my heart in these matters? Do I want to co-labor with Jesus to improve the lives of hurting people by praying for the sick, injured and those in pain?

6

"The Big Yes"

In the weeks that followed Veracruz I was becoming more and more open to God using me. My wife and I were volunteers at a children's center where at risk youth resided. A few weeks before Christmas the children's center donated a whole bunch of toys to our nonprofit, because they knew that we would give them to poor kids in San Diego. At that time I had been talking to a friend who owned a home in a poorer section of San Diego called Barrio Logan. I got the idea that we could bring these toys into her neighborhood and do an outreach there.

So we picked a date and made up flyers to be passed around the neighborhood. And although I had done outreach in the past I sensed that this one was to be different. I felt that God wanted to show me that He really did want to do the miraculous in San Diego as He did in Mexico. So when I composed the flyer I felt it was time to be bold about God's intentions to heal and do miracles. On the flyer I put "Come to receive free toys and if you have any sickness or injuries or pain in your body come to be healed." Some more risky business, but my confidence in God was increasing.

On the day of the outreach we arrived at the location a couple of hours ahead of the scheduled start time and gave kids in the neighborhood a few bucks to pass out flyers. We set up our tables with toys, prayed for God to do what He had done in Mexico and started looking for people to pray for. This was the most intentional thing in the area of healing I had ever done in the United States. God was about to answer big-time.

Before the scheduled time to begin a neighborhood lady came by just inquiring about what was going on. I told her exactly what was going on that we were going to give away toys and pray for the sick and I asked her if she had any need for prayer. She appeared to be in her early 40s and told us that when she was young she was a gymnast and that she had always love gymnastics. But in her teenage years she blew out both of her knees and although the doctors did all they could she had to quit gymnastics and had to walk in pain right up to the present.

I offered to pray for her and when she said yes a couple of my friends and I gathered around her and began. Within a minute or so she started to tremble and perspire and could not stand up. We got her chair and continued to pray for her knees, although God was obviously doing something else. She continued to shake, perspire and then she began to cry and when I asked her if she was doing good or bad she said "very good." I had seen this before when the loving, comforting presence of the Holy Spirit comes upon a person. I was glad for her because I knew that the Lord was touching her heart.

I asked her how her knees were doing but she replied that although they were the same she was feeling really, really good and was experiencing deep peace, warmth and the presence of God. She left and we didn't see her again that day. But, a few days later my friend who lives next door to her said that she came running to her house quite happy that her knees were totally healed and that she didn't have any pain! The comment she made speaks volumes about the reason to go after healing and the miraculous, she said to my friend that she had been somewhat of a believer for a long time but, she said "Now I **really** believe in God!"

Although this prayer session didn't result in immediate physical healing it resulted in an immediate experience of the love of God and then the physical healing came later. What I am learning about prayer times like this is that God likes to do things His way and has good reasons for doing what He does. I refuse to limit Him.

Healing the whole person

In this case it was obvious that God wanted to touch her deeply on an emotional level by immersing her in His presence and power. I have seen tears, shaking and perspiring many times over the years. The reason why she couldn't stand up was that the deep peace and power of His presence simply overloaded her circuits. God was giving her an encounter with Himself and His amazing love for her, an encounter which affected areas of her life that only she would know about but which she would not forget. This emotional encounter was as important to the Father as the physical healing of her knees. Here was His child, wounded, sad and hurting emotionally as well as physically. God showed her that He cared about her whole person.

Some people say that we don't have a need for these emotional experiences and manifestations today; after all we have the Bible. I say we need much more of these kinds of emotional experiences and physical manifestations, yes, more than ever. Why? Because theology can never replace the intimate relationship with God that our spirit, soul and body craves. Yes we need to believe theologically in a God and Father but we also need a here and now Daddy who will pick us up, put us in His lap, wrap His arms around us and show us how much He loves us. Yes we need to theologically believe in Jesus as Savior and Lord but we also need a here and now friend who we can talk to and be with as a friend. Yes we need to theologically believe in a Holy Spirit to guide us into all truth and show us more about Jesus, but we very much also need a here and now Comforter who will comfort us in all of life's crappy situations.

A little later on in the outreach, a man from across the street sent one of his kids to get us to come to his house after he heard that some people were getting healed. So I took a couple of friends with me and went to see him. He was sitting down on his sofa in a corset-like upper body brace that went from under his arms to the tip of his tailbone. He told us that he had been in an accident, injured his back and had been like this for several weeks. He couldn't work at all and it was very difficult for him to move without severe pain. He was obviously worried about his physical and financial future.

We prayed for him intensively for 15 to 20 minutes without any obvious improvement. We made sure his kids had some toys and some clothes and we said goodbye with words of encouragement for him to believe in Jesus and His power to heal him. About two weeks later he told my friend that he had been completely healed over a period of several days after we prayed and was back to work! This was an example of what I have learned (and am still learning) about not going by what I see. I have chosen to make a point of walking away from a prayer session believing. And I have come to discover that many people will be healed instantly, and some will be healed over time, my part being to pray and believe.

The rest of the day in Barrio Logan went great. We prayed for several people who reported being free of pain from injuries and sicknesses. We gave away toys and clothes to thankful people. And of course we led several people to Jesus! I was beginning to see that this was more of what "normal Christianity" should look like; giving people all of what God wanted them to have along with forgiveness of sins and eternal life.

For me this was proof that God did want to do in San Diego what I had seen him do in Mexico!

What really took place?

In retrospect, the essence of what we did that day was again actually demonstrating the Kingdom of God and the will of God in the here and now as it is in Heaven. God was more fully downloading to me the fact that my gospel/good news which I had preached for the previous 20 years was great and wonderful but not complete. The good news of the Kingdom of God is more complete. This is the gospel that Jesus and His early followers preached. The terms the Kingdom, the Kingdom of God and the Kingdom of Heaven is used over 125 times in the New Testament.

I highly recommend any books by John Wimber. He was a pastor and teacher who founded Vineyard Christian Fellowship International during the 70s, 80s and 90s. Over 1500 churches were established all over the world because of his leadership and teaching. His teachings have influenced the emergence of a healing culture which has flowed into the 21st century. Here's what he has to say about the Kingdom of God in his book "Power Healing":

> In the New Testament Jesus always combined healing with proclaiming the Kingdom of God. Through healing the sick, Jesus defeated satan and demonstrated His rule... at the beginning of His public ministry, Jesus announced that the Kingdom of God was near (Mark 1:15) and immediately begin healing the sick and casting out demons. When He healed a demon possessed man who was blind and mute, He told the Pharisees, "if I drive out demons by the Spirit of God then the Kingdom of God has come upon you" (Matthew 12:28). In Luke 17:21 He proclaimed that the Kingdom of God, His rule, was within us, and in 1 Corinthians 10:11 Paul writes that "the fulfillment of the ages has come to us." So Jesus brought the age to come into our present age. (Galatians 1:4; Ephesians 1:21)

The gospel/good news I had preached for so many years did not include the things that Jesus included in His gospel...the gospel of the Kingdom. In my earlier efforts to fulfill the great commission I gave away only what I had learned. I didn't give away the same gospel that the early disciples preached and gave away. Through the things that happened to me in Tijuana, Veracruz, and now Barrio Logan I was coming to learn that God wanted me to include in my preaching of the gospel of His Kingdom healing, freedom from demonic oppression and miracles, as well as forgiveness of sins resulting in eternal life.

Very gently the Lord was showing me that I had diminished what He wanted to do for people.

I had not placed the same value on the Kingdom of God as Jesus had.

I had not placed the same value on healings and miracles that Jesus did.

I needed to repent (change my mind) about these things and preach the same gospel Jesus preached.

Yes I have given many people the most wonderful thing that they could have: salvation, eternal life and a relationship with Jesus but I neglected to give them the fullness of what Jesus wanted to give them. In the next chapter we will be talking about this Gospel of the Kingdom of God and how God wants to use us so that **this "Gospel of the Kingdom" is preached in the entire world before the end comes.**

About the sovereignty of God

I would like you to think about something. Yes, God is sovereign and He allows sickness disease and pain in the world. But God was sovereignly allowing sickness in the days of Jesus wasn't He? Yet Jesus didn't look at the fact that God was allowing sickness and do nothing about it. He didn't say to anyone "well, you know, God is sovereign and if He has allowed this, you need to stay sick." No, he proceeded to heal even though God in His sovereignty had allowed sickness.

We must not lump together everything bad that happens in the world around us and especially to our friends and family under the heading "the sovereignty of God." If we do this we risk unnecessary sickness, pain and suffering. Not everything that is allowed under the sovereignty of God is the will of God. This was clearly shown by Jesus wasn't it?

7

"The Gospel of the Kingdom of God"

"If I cast out devils by the finger of God then the Kingdom of God has come upon you"

"Heal the sick there and tell them that the Kingdom of God is at hand"

Before I go any further into my story I must take a long pause and talk about some critical things. I must go back to the beginning of my excursion into the supernatural in Tijuana, Mexico. Before that weekend outreach in 2000, when the Lord spoke to me about declaring His Kingdom, during my times of prayer I was saying to Him that I wanted to see the same things that took place in the early church. The desire of my heart that I put before the Lord was a desire to find out how healings and miracles could accompany my gospel/good news as it accompanied the gospel of the early church. What was really amazing was that God did not hesitate to say "declare My Kingdom and I will come..."

But, as my friend and Pastor Ed Noble would say, "A question that is begging to be answered" is why God said this and not some other things in response to my question. He didn't say to pray for the sick or anoint with oil or lay hands on people or declare eternal life in Jesus or many other things that may have brought about a demonstration of His power. No, He said "Declare my Kingdom and I will come." I'm glad God doesn't waste words. He so knows what is exactly needed for any situation. In this case what was needed was a declaration of His Kingdom! What needed to take place was a bold declaration that the Kingdom of God was at hand, that it was here and now, that the rulership and dominion of God controls everything and that the works of the devil would have to yield to the power of the Kingdom. His Kingdom was to be released through me, a simple ordinary believer and follower of Jesus. This was to bring about the signs that accompanied the early church. And when I did that in Tijuana and when I did it everywhere else since, healings and/or miracles took place.

Isn't this what Jesus did?

> ...And Jesus went about all Galilee, teaching in their synagogues, preaching **the Gospel of the Kingdom, and healing all kinds of sickness and all kinds of disease among the people.** (Matt4: 17, 9:35)

Do you see the combination of healing and the preaching of the Kingdom? He wasn't talking about a Kingdom that was in the future He was talking about a Kingdom that was in the here and now which He, King Jesus, had brought to Earth. He said, "If I cast out demons by the spirit of God, surely the Kingdom of God **has** come upon you." (Matt 12:28). So He not only preached about the Kingdom but He demonstrated that it was at hand by healing the sick, raising the dead and casting out demons. He spent a whole bunch of time talking about the Kingdom. He went into great detail about it and its importance to the world and us as believers. He said, "I must preach the Kingdom of God to the other cities also, because for this purpose I have been sent."

It was so important that He called it His main purpose for coming!

In describing the Kingdom He said it was the most desirable thing for a human being to attain. He described it as a rare pearl and a treasure that a person would give everything to have. He took great pains to communicate to anyone who would listen, the importance of seeking, receiving, preaching about and demonstrating the Kingdom.

The great transfer of power and authority

I think the most wonderful thing about the Kingdom is that Jesus not only brought it and demonstrated it, but He made it available to all. In fact He gave it to His disciples. He said "I will give you the keys of the Kingdom of Heaven and whatever you bind on earth will be bound in Heaven and whatever you loose on earth will be loosed in Heaven." (Matt 16:19) In fact He said that it was the Fathers' **good pleasure** to give His children the Kingdom. (Luke 12:32) (Luke 22:29). **In actuality the**

great commission included preaching the Kingdom of God and healing the sick. *"He sent them to preach the Kingdom of God and to heal the sick."* Again it was the combination of preaching the Kingdom and demonstration by healing.

So, He transfers power and authority to the 12 as stated in Luke 9:1 which says, "Then He called his 12 disciples together and gave them power and authority over all demons and to cure diseases." In Luke 10:19 He says, "I give you the authority to trample on serpents and scorpions and over all the power of the enemy and nothing shall by any means hurt you."

But, it was not just for Jesus and the 12; he sent 70 more to do the same thing. In Luke 10 Jesus appoints 70 others and tells them to go out into the cities and "heal the sick there, and say to them, 'the Kingdom of God has come near to you.'" And then Paul continued (Acts 19:8). And others like Stephen and Philip followed suit. "...when they believed Philip as he preached the things concerning the Kingdom of God..." (Acts 8: 6-12).

So what happened when Jesus and all of His followers preached the Kingdom of God? There was a demonstration that the rule, dominion, authority and power of King Jesus and the Kingdom of God was mightier than the works of the devil. Who did Jesus heal? "All who were oppressed of the devil." (Acts 10:38) Who did Jesus set free? The demon possessed and oppressed because He came to destroy the works of the devil. Therefore when the Kingdom is preached and demonstrated God basically shows who is really in charge. God takes back territory from the devil. God demonstrates that He and He alone is the last word regarding the works of the devil. In essence Jesus was saying; tell the people that their liberation is here and the strongholds and bondages that the powers of darkness have kept them subject to for so long are broken!

Wasn't this the essence of the mission of Jesus? Jesus' mission and ours are clearly outlined in this passage:

He went to Nazareth, where He had been brought up, and on the Sabbath day He went into the synagogue, as was His custom. And He stood up to read. The scroll of the prophet Isaiah was handed to Him. Unrolling it **He found the place** where it is written "the Spirit of the Lord is upon Me, because He has anointed Me to preach good news to the poor. He has sent Me to proclaim freedom for the prisoners and recovery of sight for the blind, to release the oppressed, to proclaim the year of the Lord's favor. (Luke 4)

Notice it says "**He found the place.**" I think Jesus took the whole scroll of the prophet Isaiah and searched for this passage so that He could intentionally proclaim what His mission was in coming to the earth. He wanted to make it very clear what the will of His Father in Heaven was for hurting, broken and captive people in the world. In essence I think Jesus was saying there's a new sheriff in town, things are going to change, the corrupt mayor and all his cronies have to go and the domination of the kingdom of darkness is at an end!

To me the good news of the Kingdom was that the poor will be helped, the brokenhearted would be healed, the prisoners of satan will be free, the blind are to be given spiritual and physical sight, and those oppressed by demonic forces are to be released. Jesus threw down the gauntlet and said to the devil "okay, the time has come we're going to get it on, we're going to see whose kingdom is the most powerful."

Remember the Tijuana story? When I declared to those people gathered there on that weekend that the Kingdom of God was at hand and that He would demonstrate His power, dominion and rulership over the powers of darkness it was like a big "yes" was said by the Lord. I really believe there was a big smile on my Father's face when I said those words. And why not, they were words of Jesus and the early church. He liked them then and likes them now. They were the words of freedom, deliverance and healing. The will of God as is in Heaven was waiting to be released. And when it was spoken over those people, the connection was made, the pipeline was opened, the switch was thrown and Heaven came to earth for many poor, captive and imprisoned people on that patch of dirt in Tijuana.

They have their holy books also

There are many philosophies and religions in the world. There are many "gods" that people can choose. There are many books that are regarded as holy books and word of God type books. So, why should people believe in our book and Jesus? Seriously, why should people believe that He is the only way to eternal life in Heaven? In the world we live in today people have the freedom to choose the God, the philosophy or the religion that suits them. Sometimes the persuasion gospel just doesn't cut it.

To make my point I will tell you a true story about a man named T. L. Osborne. He was radically born again in the first half of the 20th century. He immediately wanted to tell the world about Jesus and felt led to go to India to do so. When he got there, over and over again he would debate with the people and religious leaders. He would try to persuade them through the Scriptures that Jesus was the way. But what he got as a response was basically this from most of the people: "You have your book and we have our book. You believe in your book and we believe in our book. Why should we change our mind and believe in your book and this Jesus you are talking about." Not one person came to Jesus over a several month period of time. He left India very disillusioned.

But when he came back to the United States he went to a meeting held by a preacher named William Branham. There he saw the gospel of the Kingdom preached and the signs following. People all around him were being healed and the preacher was talking about the healings being proof of Jesus being the Son of God, Savior and Messiah. He sensed the Lord saying to him "this is how they will believe, preach this way."

He determined to do it and returned to India with overwhelming success and was used by God in great evangelistic and healing outreaches there and all over the world.

The point is, he was dealing with the same people as before except now they saw and experienced the power of God.

Isn't it our responsibility to give the people of the world **all** the reasons we can to believe in Jesus? Words only go so far. **If we cannot present a real and powerful here and now God who can do something about their deepest needs in every area of life; I we cannot present a Savior who can heal their sicknesses, diseases, oppressions, heart aches and sins, then we are doing a disservice to them and to our Lord.**

People need to be affirmed and encouraged in their life's journey. They need to know that God cares for them in practical ways and cares for every day stuff in their lives.

Personal application of the Kingdom, power and authority

As mentioned before, in Luke 10:19 Jesus told the 70, after they had returned in victory over demonic forces, "behold, I give you authority to trample on serpents and scorpions, and over all the power of the enemy, and nothing shall by any means hurt you."

One of the biggest lies of the devil over many centuries has been that the ordinary believer doesn't have any power over the harmful stuff that comes into their lives. When sickness or pain comes we primarily look for some natural reason for it. We'll say things like "Oh, the flu is going around so I guess I'm going to get it." And when the first symptom comes we fold and accept it. But, what did Jesus mean by "**nothing** shall by any means hurt you." I think we can safely say that when Jesus says nothing He means nothing, as far as sickness and the demonic are concerned.

This should say to us that when something is hurting or harming us we should consider the possibility of the demonic behind it. Jesus referred to the demonic as serpents and scorpions under the power of the enemy. So, is it safe to assume that cancer and other diseases have their origins in the demonic? Especially given the fact that Scripture says that God **only** gives good gifts?

We need to ask ourselves the questions "can sickness and disease be a good gift? Is cancer a good gift? Are any of the other debilitating, wasting and painful diseases and afflictions gifts from God? Is God good and does He give good gifts or not?

If we conclude that He only gives good gifts then the diseases and afflictions mentioned above probably are from other sources and perhaps demonic in origin.

In James 4:7 it says, "Therefore submit to God. Resist the devil and he will flee from you."

I believe that many hurtful and harmful things that come our way can be resisted in the name of Jesus and that it is **possible** to actually avoid being hurt and harmed by many things. But, it requires the exercise of our God given power and authority. **We** have the responsibility to resist, to say no, and refuse. We can either allow the enemy to defeat us or not allow.

I have come up with a phrase that I use for myself and share with others. The phrase is **"Refuse to sign for the package!"** What this means is that if a person came to my front door with a package and a label on it that says "sickness, disease and pain inside," I would naturally say "no thanks, that doesn't belong to me, it's not my package, I'm not signing for it."

Over the course of recent months I have had a good measure of success doing this. I am not allowing myself to fall into the trap of saying that because I am getting older I should be subject to infirmity or other hurtful or harmful things. So, what I do when **the first** symptom comes my way I resist in the name of Jesus and refuse to sign for the package. Even if I know of a reason why it should be there, I refuse it (IE it's Flu season).

I am beginning to lock into the life abundant that Jesus promised. And just like everything else I don't have it down pat nor am I an expert on it. But in recent months there must have been at least a dozen different symptoms, aches and pains that I have refused in the name Jesus. And they have all disappeared. I have refused to sign for all those packages.

I don't believe it is foolish to take Jesus' words to heart that say "nothing by any means shall harm you." and, act on them by exercising the power and authority we had in and through His name.

Jesus hated sickness and oppression and we must learn to hate them also. View sickness and the things that harm and oppress as an enemy to be defeated by the power and authority we have in and through the mighty name that is above every name! If we don't learn to resist we risk being overcome by the evil one. Don't sign for that harmful package the devil is trying to deliver to you!

Please understand I am not talking about the suffering related to being a believer in Jesus or because of the gospel. Persecution, rejection, beatings, imprisonment and even martyrdom are common sufferings that are taking place all around the world today. But, I refuse to include sickness or disease in the sufferings that Jesus told us that we should expect because Jesus didn't include them. He viewed them as oppressions of the enemy to be defeated!

No hiccups in heaven

Fast-forward to the present. I am writing these words after returning from taking my car to the mechanic. This was the second time for the same problem, so I wasn't in a highly spiritual mood. While waiting for my car to be repaired I went to a taco shop. A girl and two guys in their early 20s came in the shop and were talking about hiccups that Reina, the girl had. They were having fun joking around about the different methods to get rid of hiccups; drinking water upside down, holding your breath etc. in fact they asked me if I ever heard of one method of curing hiccups. I said no and sat down to wait for my order.

While sitting there for about a minute a thought came into my mind. "Jesus can heal hiccups." My mind quickly went back and forth…Hiccups? Jesus? Hiccups! I agreed with the thought and decided to take a risk and see if it was a God thought.

I asked the girl's name and said something like "I know a way for you to be free of hiccups without you having to do anything." When the words came out of my mouth I was a bit surprised. They were words that I don't think I would have thought up at the time, because it involved some risk. So I made a quick decision that it most probably was a word from God. Reina asked how this could happen and I said "what if I prayed for you and the hiccups went away?" One of them replied "what if you do what?" I repeated myself. She quickly said yes and I prayed a simple prayer for her asking Jesus to reveal His love to her and commanding the hiccups to stop.

About 10 seconds later she shouted "this is crazy!" I asked what was crazy and she said "it's crazy, I don't have the hiccups anymore, I haven't had hiccups since I was a kid and all of a sudden all morning I have them, but I don't have them anymore!" To be honest I would have been happier if she had waited a little longer to say she didn't have the hiccups. There was a little doubt creeping into my mind. But as we talked time passed and I knew God had cured her, so I told her more about God's love for her and that Jesus was even concerned about her hiccups and that maybe the hiccups were there so that she could experience the love of God. The two guys didn't have anything to say.

I got my food and joined her at a table. She said again with a confused look on her face "this is crazy." I went on to share with her how Jesus cared about more than just her hiccups; He cared about her whole life.

While I was talking to her I was asking the Lord for a word of encouragement for her. This is what is called a word of knowledge. It is referred to in 1 Corinthians 12:4-11. This is usually some insight into a person's life which results in them realizing that God knows and cares about them. This may have been what occurred between Jesus and the woman at the well. It resulted in her and the whole town being very interested in Jesus.

I thought I heard inside of me the word art or arts. I told her about this and she said again something like "this is crazy, I love the arts but I like dance especially, someday I would like to teach dancing and choreography." She was looking at me like I was a psychic so I explained a little bit more about God caring about every part of her life and especially about the gifts and talents she had for the arts. I asked her if she knew Jesus and she said she didn't.

I reviewed with her how God loved and cared for her enough to cure her hiccups and encourage her about her talents and her future. I briefly shared the gospel of salvation with her and asked her if she would like to ask Jesus into her life, have her sins forgiven, have eternal life and a relationship with this Jesus who loved her and cared so much about her. She immediately said yes. I was a bit taken aback that there was not even one objection. So just to make sure I asked her again and explained little bit more about what Jesus did for her on the cross and how to have forgiveness of sins and eternal life. When I asked if she would like to pray with me to ask Jesus into her life, she again immediately said yes. We prayed and she prayed and God welcomed her into His family!

At this point her boyfriend Deshawn came back to the table and I introduced myself to him and just started asking about his job and other chitchat stuff. Reina said to me, "Why don't you do that thing for him too." And she started telling her boyfriend about the words that I spoke to her. I explained that I was not a psychic but that God might have an encouraging word for him. I talked with him for a minute or two when the word baseball came to me. When I asked him if he was really into sports Reina freaked out again saying "this is crazy, he loves sports." When I mentioned baseball he said "yeah I like baseball but I like basketball even more, but I love all sports." I also told him what I had told Reina, explaining what his girlfriend just did about Jesus and I basically shared the same thing I shared with her and when I asked him if he also would like to ask Jesus into his life and have his sins forgiven he immediately said yes also. Inside of me I was saying this is too good to be true, it was so easy.

Reina and her boyfriend asked their third friend, Jason, to come over so that I could do the same thing for him. I was feeling a little under pressure at this point and I said to them something like I don't really do anything, I just try to hear from Jesus what He wants them to know and I reiterated that I was not a psychic. I told Jason that I couldn't come up with a word for him but that Jesus might. I decided to just chat with him for a few minutes and then I got a strong word about his mother. I had the sense that his mother was a believer and a strong Christian and asked if this was true and if she took him to church when he was young. He said yes to it all.

At this point he's looking at me with no expression on his face whatsoever. I'm thinking he's just not buying what I was saying. Then I got the word electronics. So I asked him if he was interested in electronics or the technology field. He said he was very interested. I think at this point Reina added another "this is crazy" because she knew about his interest in the tech field. So I shared with him and the others that God really cares about their future and that He was encouraging them to pursue their dreams, gifts and talents. I asked Jason if he would like to do what his other two friends had done. He also quickly responded yes.

So, I also led him in a prayer to receive the Lord. I then shared with all of them to be seeking after the Lord and His will for their lives, to read the New Testament to find out more about Jesus and to hang out with other Christians and go to church. I gave them my card and told them to call me if they had any questions or if they wanted to come to a home fellowship group that we have at our house. They sounded very interested.

What really took place?

Isn't it amazing that God will take something as silly as hiccups and use it to express His love? But, how does the Gospel of the Kingdom fit into the story?

God demonstrated His role as a good King and one who cares about people. He showed these three young people that His Kingdom power and love were in the here and now and just for them. He willingly had an encounter with them and freely gave them good things out of His love for them. I'm not sure they would have been as willingly open to the Lord without the demonstration of the things He did and said to them. I believe that God was so interested in these three young people that He was pretty much ready and willing to use anything to touch their lives. For God, His Kingdom rule over hiccups was very important!

Salvation is much more than having your sins forgiven and going to Heaven. John Wimber, in his book "Power Healing" speaks about this when he did a study on the words salvation and healing. It seems that they are strongly connected in one root word. He says:

> Another Greek verb for "healing," is Sozo (its intensive form, diasozo) is used in stories of healing 16 times. What is interesting about Sozo, which is taken from an Aramaic term, is that it has the twofold meaning of "to make alive" and "to make healthy."

In Mark 3:4, Jesus, on the occasion of healing on the Sabbath a man with a crippled hand, asked the Pharisees, "which is lawful on the Sabbath to do good or to do evil, to save life or to kill?" The phrase "to save life" is - psuchen sozai-which implies spiritual as well as physical salvation.
He quotes author John Wilkinson:

> It is clear that Sozo's wide application in the Gospels indicates that the Christian concept of healing and the Christian concept of salvation overlap to a degree which varies in different situations, but are never completely separable. Healing of the body is never purely physical and the salvation of the soul is never purely spiritual, but both are combined in **the total deliverance of the whole man,** a deliverance which is foreshadowed and illustrated in the healing miracles of Jesus in the Gospels.

Some in the modern day western church have unfortunately come to the conclusion that salvation is limited to the forgiveness of sins and eternal life. The truth and reality is, as far as Jesus and the early church was concerned, salvation included life, wholeness, deliverance from demonic oppression and healing.

As my excursion into God's command to "declare My Kingdom," continued I was sensing over and over that God strongly wanted the fullness of **this** gospel of the Kingdom of God preached and I was to take the risks and scorn involved with preaching it the way He wanted. He was strongly indicating that there was no going back and no options for me at this point. So this became the theme of the rest of my life. And although I was very glad about it at this time, I knew many obstacles lay ahead.

8

Another confirmation and on to jail

"I have come to declare freedom to prisoners and release to captives"

After my experiences in Barrio Logan I was committed to carrying out God's mandate to bring His Kingdom and healing and delivering power to people. The confirmation I got in the barrio led to another confirmation which I really didn't need, but one that God gave anyway. The following year around Christmas time we received more free gifts to give away. I decided to do another outreach in another poorer area of San Diego called Linda Vista. This was a community of Hispanic and Vietnamese people. We decided to reach out to the Hispanic people in this area.

Now I was committed to becoming a "full service gospel provider." We basically did the same thing we did in the barrio. We handed out fliers to the community offering gifts for the children and offering healing prayer for any kind of problem that people were having. This time we had a face painting tent and a clown for the kids and some Christmas/worship music. More than 200 people arrived that day and I asked my team to meet and greet the people as they came to the area of the park where we were meeting. I told them to immediately ask what the people's needs were and to pray accordingly. We all waded into the crowd with the expectation of the goodness and will of God showing up.

After I felt that my friends had enough time to pray for those in need I took the microphone and welcomed the crowd and asked people who were prayed for if anyone was healed or freed from pain. Just like in the barrio several people raise their hands and told the story of how God had met their needs by taking away pain and/or touching them emotionally. After having some of them give their testimonies I talked a bit about the Kingdom and gave an invitation to know Jesus personally. It was another really good day and another confirmation of the direction that God was taking me.

On to jail

In the days to follow I just continued to make myself available to the Lord's leading. A good friend, Larry Johnson, invited me to join him in ministering in the central jail in downtown San Diego and in an adult detention facility near the Mexican border. After the application process was completed I went with great expectancy to these jails. And like Paul in first Corinthians I determined that my message and my preaching were not going to be just in a mode of persuasion with words about Jesus but in demonstration of the Holy Spirit and power.

In fact Paul's letter to the Corinthians and especially what he had to say in chapter 2 made a very strong case for the combination of the preaching of the gospel and a demonstration of power.

There is good reason to believe that Paul had left Athens somewhat disappointed with the response of the people there. After meeting with the Council of Elders on Mars Hill and trying to persuade them about Jesus and the resurrection of the dead, Acts 17:32-34 says: "When they heard about the resurrection of the dead, some of them sneered, but others said, we want to hear you again on this subject. At that, Paul left the council. **A few men** became followers of Paul and believed..."

In Acts 18:1 it says "**after this** Paul left Athens and went to Corinth." But even at the beginning of his ministry in Corinth he was reasoning with the Jews who pretty much dismissed him and we see his frustration in Acts 18:6. "But when the Jews opposed Paul and became abusive he shook out his clothes in protest and said to them, "your blood be on your own head! I am clear of my responsibility...from now on I will go to the Gentiles."

Some believe that Paul was shook by the unsuccessful verbal appeal to both the Athenians and the Jews at Corinth and determined that it should be different when he went to the Gentiles. In 1 Corinthians 2 it looks like Paul had taken a change of direction in his preaching. In going to the Gentiles it could be reasoned that Paul knew he couldn't use persuasion as he had tried to do with the Jews. How much of the Scriptures would the Gentiles know and understand? How much of the prophecies concerning Jesus would they be willing to accept? It looks like he was not going to only use words of persuasion with the Gentile Corinthians, but that he was going to demonstrate the power of the Holy Spirit.

In chapter 2 of first Corinthians it's clear that he was addressing Gentiles. He says:

When I came to you brothers, I did not come with eloquence or superior wisdom as I proclaimed to you the testimony about God. For I resolved to know nothing while I was with you except Jesus Christ and Him crucified. I came to you in weakness and fear and with much trembling.

The weakness, fear and trembling could be attributed to a somewhat unsuccessful Athens evangelistic campaign and his unsuccessful persuasive tactics with the Jews in Corinth. Paul could have been afraid that the same thing would happen with the Gentiles in Corinth.

He goes on to say:

....my message and my preaching were not with wise and persuasive words but with a **demonstration of the Spirits power so that your faith might not rest on men's wisdom, but on God's power.**

Please take a long look at that last sentence. Ponder it if you will. Paul is saying that he was determined not to try to use wise and persuasive words to try to convince the Gentiles about Jesus. To me it seems that he was going to preach differently than he had previously and allow the Spirit of God to demonstrate His power. It seems he would rather let the power of God speak louder than persuasive words. In fact he goes on to say in essence that he would **rather have people's faith rest in the power** of God than in men's words! **Please think about this! He wanted these new believers faith to rest in God's power, the power of the Holy Spirit. Paul, who was probably the most educated and eloquent of Jesus' disciples, decides that his highly educated and eloquent words were not sufficient to bring the Gentiles fully into the Kingdom of God and to salvation.** He wanted them to have something **powerful** to experience and remember at the same time they heard the words about Jesus. He wanted them to have a **power encounter** with the Spirit of the living God. He wanted their faith to rest in that **power encounter.** He didn't want them just persuaded into the Kingdom; he wanted them **powered** into the Kingdom. This power encounter would stick with them long after persuasive words were spoken!

Someone said that if we can talk a person into a decision for Jesus, someone might be able to talk them out of that decision. I'm not sure to what extent this is true, but why not give people power to believe in as well as the truth of Jesus' death, burial and resurrection. I don't know about you, but I'm determined to continue preaching it the way Jesus and the disciples and Paul and others preached it. With words and power!

So, before going into the jails, I told my friend Larry that this is what I would be doing if I went with him. He told me to go for it. And God showed up in the jails just as He showed up in Barrio Logan and Linda Vista.

The story of scary Claude

In the jails we would usually have about an hour and a half with the men. We were assigned to do a church/chapel service. My heart really went out to these men each time we gathered. Although every one of them were criminals, I saw them as misguided, beaten down and lied to by the enemy. Although they were offenders they were also victims, and very much sheep without a shepherd.

They came out to the meetings for various reasons. A few were hoping for a "get out of jail card." What I mean by this is that some of them hoped that if they turned to God and came to Chapel that God would get them out of lock up. A few just came to get out of their cell but most of them were sincerely wanting God's help in their situation and sincerely wanting change in their lives. What they didn't know is that God wanted them to be free on the inside, spiritually and emotionally free in the way that only Jesus could accomplish. It seemed that for many saying "the sinner's prayer" just wasn't going to cut it. Most of them had been there and done that.

In talking to these guys I was astounded that most of them had either made a decision for Jesus in the past or had been raised in a Christian or church environment. I would often inquire of the Lord asking why these men were in jail if they had a background which included Jesus and the church. I was also asking how He wanted to affect change in their lives in our services. What I felt the Lord show me to do was basically obey my assignment. Perhaps these men never had a power encounter with a here and now Jesus. He reminded me: "Declare my Kingdom, and I will come." I was determined to offer as many men as possible a message and a faith based on the power of the Spirit, as well as words.

Doing this in the jails was somewhat scary and I was a little shaky at the beginning. The thoughts that were going through my mind during the first couple of visits were pretty negative. Would there be power, would God back me up, can these men be affected in a dramatic and powerful way, haven't they heard it all before in other church or prison services? I knew that most had heard the gospel of Jesus and eternal life. I knew that most had been to many church or prison chapel services. Could anything we did make things different for them? Once again I had to wade through fear and the lies of the enemy to do what God had called me to do.

At one of the first services a big, burly, bearded, tattooed and scary looking guy named Claude was there. I preached and declared the Kingdom of God and about Jesus being the same yesterday, today and forever and I told stories of what He had done in Tijuana, Veracruz, Barrio Logan and Linda Vista, I told them that He would do the same now. I remember preaching about how God wanted them to not just believe the words that we spoke but also to experience His power.

I asked who had injuries and pain and Claude raised his hand. Claude was saying that he had blown out his shoulder while trying to bench-press an enormous amount of weight in the iron yard of the jail. Uh Oh! Was it my imagination or was his demeanor saying "so, preacher, you think this Jesus can heal my shoulder?" Although I sensed a challenge I also sensed that Claude really wanted to believe. But, although the chapel service was a very safe place to be in the jail, I had a fleeting picture of Claude grabbing me with his good arm after his other arm didn't get healed.

But thank God, after prayer, all of Claude's pain left his shoulder and he was able to lift it above his head for the first time in weeks! Along with a few four letter bombs Claude was happily telling about how good he felt and how surprised he was. I had seen this before. This big scary guy was now like a child who had just gotten the best Christmas present ever. The look on his face said it all. Claude's healing spoke volumes to the other guys. Claude obviously had some juice in the jail and his healing testified to others a reality of the here and now Jesus!

Inwardly I sighed a big sigh of relief, was thanking Jesus and dancing. Once again God had my back and demonstrated that I was not alone in this process. **Co-laboring with Christ was taking on a whole new meaning. He was showing me that He would be with me in some of the scariest and riskiest situations.** You know, no matter how many times I pray for the sick and how confident I am, I too am gratefully surprised when the miraculous happens right in front of my eyes. It is a thrill that I don't want to get used to.

An instant discipleship class

For me and for Claude the best part was yet to come. The following week Claude showed up with a few of his friends from the cell block. I wondered if he "gently persuaded" them to be there. I preached for a while and ask those who were sick or in pain to come forward for prayer. About six responded. I also asked for those who wanted to be used by God to pray for people to come forward. Two men responded, but Claude was not one of them. I shared with the men a little more about giving away what we had received from the Lord and again invited those to come forward who wanted to pray for others, but Claude still didn't respond. So I just asked him to come forward anyway and he reluctantly agreed.

There was a man up front who had no feeling from the elbow down in his right arm. This is because he shot up drugs in that arm. Although Claude only became a follower of Jesus a few weeks earlier I asked him to pray for the man but he resisted saying he didn't know how to do it. I told him to pray the way he saw me pray for his shoulder. I left him to do that and turned my attention to some of the men on the other side of the room.

After just a couple of minutes I heard the guy with no feeling in his lower arm shouting "I can feel my arm, I can feel my arm!" I turned around and sure enough this man reported that all the feeling had returned to his arm. Once again I was surprised but didn't show it. Claude was totally confused about the whole thing. But he continued praying for the man who had pain in both his knees. His knees got healed also! I went on to talk to the guys about how God is not looking for experts or super holy, religious people to be used to pray for and help others, He is simply looking for followers of Jesus who are available. Claude was one of them.

Several other men who were prayed for that night were healed also. Once again I was able to point to these things and say this is the Jesus who wants to be a part of your life and who you should follow with your whole heart. Several guys prayed with me at the end of the evening, some for the first time and some to renew their waning commitment to the Lord

But, what's to say about Claude? No 10 week discipleship training course? No certificate from a seminary. No ordination. A criminal in jail? Certainly God couldn't use someone like this could He? I'll leave you to decide, but consider this:

Wasn't this sort of the way Jesus did things? He selected some men who weren't qualified at all; some men who would later even betray and disown him; some men who would want to call fire down from Heaven to destroy people and some men who would not believe He was raised from the dead when told. He took these men and modeled healing and the miraculous. And then He let them do it while He watched and critiqued. And then later He would send them out do it on their own. Thanks for the *four step model Jesus! Let's see, didn't He say **anyone** who believed in Him would do the works that He did?

Claude wrote me a couple of letters after his experiences with God in our chapel services. Here are some excerpts:

John,

Hello my brother... I am so happy that God has begun the work of rebuilding my life and my family... I am just happy to know and have met you... I am proud of you and I wish you were my father...I grew up in the roughest part of San Diego...I've survived adversity and I've been a drug addict since I was 12 years old. I have five prison numbers, four in California and one in Nevada... my childhood was a nightmare and my adulthood was a big long sentence... but, it's time to stop living Claude's life for Claude and to start living Claude's life for God... wow!

There is so much to say...us meeting in Bailey Detention Center in San Diego, through you God heals my shoulder, which is still healed, we healed the guys arm and knees that crack and we healed the other guys back pain!

There is a lot of stuff that goes on around me but I try not to focus on that stuff and focus on the prize, the gift, the hope, the joy, the peace. But most of all the love. I am all alone now, my sister is gone, my mom, dad, grandparents on both sides too. My other siblings have forgotten me but at least I have God...

What affect did his exposure to the miraculous have in his life? You decide.

During the next two years working in the jails I saw God do many new and wonderful things over and over again. Here are just a few stories:

A man named Russell at Bailey Detention Center was overcome by the Holy Spirit and began sweating shaking and crying as he experienced the love and presence of God.

Russell writes:

....as for me I am blessed. I just want to thank both of you for taking time out to preach the word to us in here. Everyone here is grateful for that and for God. Since I've been here I've been going to your services and I can say each and every one of them is just awesome, just like our Lord and Savior. Praise God!

Cause I can truly say on August 28, 2006 at your service here I felt the Holy Spirit and that really made me believe there is a God... Oh, it was just so beautiful. I was filled with the Spirit, tears came down my face, joy filled my mind and I didn't want that day to be over.

When I came back to my cell block everyone was saying "Russell your face is glowing." I came in telling everyone "I was filled with the Holy Spirit." I even called my family back in New York and it was late because of the three-hour difference in time. My sister said Russell, don't you know it's 1 AM. I said oh yeah but I felt the Holy Spirit! Then I came back to my cell and wrote everyone I knew about it. If you are ever filled with the Holy Spirit, just always remember that day no matter what goes on in your life, because when I feel the devil or things just aren't going right I reflect on that wonderful day. And I just start to smile and pray! The Lord is wonderful and I'm going to do all I can to keep him in my life, I love Him just as much as He loves me and you, too!

The good news is that Russell's encounter with the Spirit of God cannot be replaced! It changed him and will help to sustain him in his faith!

One night I had Josh who had shoulder pain and Aaron who had a sore throat pray for each other and they both reported instant relief. They had never prayed for anyone in their lives!

Then there was Hugh who had an injury after he fell from a second story building and compressed discs in his back. He had pain of 6 to 7 all the time and he reported total healing. I had him pray for a new believer, Antonio, who had pain in his neck and shoulders and Antonio also reported freedom from pain.

Many of the men who had some exposure to Jesus and the church previously, had come to a new level of relationship with Him after these power encounters. They now knew someone who not only went to a cross for them 2000 years ago, but someone who was in the here and now with them and cared and loved them so much as to touch their lives deeper than they had been touched before. I believe these men will never be the same.

I feel a contentment to know that I have helped to bring them into a new and deeper relationship with Jesus. It would be just plain harder for them to fall away now, having had these experiences. And I feel they will have more of a reality of "God with us" because of them.

A couple of my most eye opening & faith challenging experiences were to come. My "view of God in the here and now" was about to be transformed even more!

9

"The thief comes to kill, steal and destroy; I have come that you might have life and life to the full."

"God is better than we think, so we need to change the way we think." Bill Johnson

The will of God is better than we believe it is

What if you came home one day and found your house ransacked and your TV, computer and jewelry gone. Even that special gift you got from your father was missing. Would you conclude that this was a thief or would you think that your father came to do this?

What if your child needed to be taught a lesson in a certain area of his life? His character needed building and his habits needed changing. Let's say all of your efforts to correct his shortcomings went unheeded. Would you break his leg to teach him? Would you poison him so that he got a wasting disease which might even result in death?

If your house was overrun by vermin or other pests, would you say to yourself, "this is just something that happens to people" and not do something about it?

These examples are pretty foolish aren't they? Who in their right mind would think of or do these things in this way. I agree, but I say, who in their **right thinking** would do these things? And yet many followers of Christ, good and decent people, devoted to God, **think this way**.

When sickness, severe lack and other life sapping things happen they often take a passive role about them and say things like "God is sovereign, He has caused or allowed these things in my life for a purpose, He probably wants to teach me something or build my character."

If the purpose of God can only be accomplished in us by Him bringing severe hardship on us, then God contradicts Himself. The Scriptures say that it is the goodness or kindness of God that leads a man to repentance. If God really wanted to build our character or cause us to repent and change our ways would He do it by slamming us against the wall or by showing us His goodness and kindness?

Let's see, God is good and the devil is bad, right? If bad things are happening I think I would rather look for the hand of the devil than look for the hand of God. I have chosen not to attribute evil to the Lord by saying that He has made me sick, caused me to have pain or injuries and brought severe hardship on me.

Allow me to take this more to an extreme through the examples mentioned above. Would the person whose house was ransacked say "this must've been done by my Father for some good reason; I'm not going to call the police or suspect a thief?"

Would the parent whose child was not behaving properly break his leg, and if that didn't work break his arm?

Would the person whose house was infested look for some reason why it was a good thing that was happening, and not do anything about it?

The point I'm trying to make is this; Jesus talks about God being a good Father and that every good and perfect gift comes down from Him and that if we asked for good gifts He would willingly give us good gifts. Jesus also said in the Scripture quoted at the beginning of this chapter "the **thief** comes to kill steal and destroy, I have come that you might have life and life to the full." Do you see the contrast? The **thief** comes to kill, not our Heavenly Father! The **thief** comes to steal, not our good Father. The **thief** comes to destroy, not our Father who came to give life to the full! In fact the Bible says **"for this reason was the Son of man manifest, that He might destroy the works of the devil." For what reason? To destroy the works of the devil.**

We need to attribute evil to the evil one and not to God!

Who's your Daddy?

Jesus came to earth. He brought His Kingdom with Him. He declared that the Kingdom of God was at hand and then He proceeded to demonstrate this by destroying the works of the devil at every turn. The Scripture says that Jesus went about **doing good and healing all who or oppressed of the devil.** To me it is clear, He went about doing good, healing and undoing the work of the devil. Sickness and disease, as far as

Jesus was concerned, was the work of the devil. Doing good, as far as Jesus was concerned, was destroying that work.

What were the works of the devil that Jesus turned around, healed or destroyed? The results of Jesus ministry was; lepers cleansed, cripples walk, deaf hear, blind see, those who died prematurely raised, the demon possessed and the demon oppressed freed. Get the analogy? Devil bad, God good. Sickness bad...health good. Oppression bad...freedom good. Can anyone show me even one time where Jesus said to a person "sorry, this disease is from your Father in Heaven to teach you something." Did He ever say to even one person "not your day pal?" "You're not holy enough" "you're too sinful." "It is not my Father's will that you be healed." Instead He kept saying, "I only do what I see my Father doing." Every time Jesus looked the Father was healing, saving, freeing and helping hurting people...overturning the work of the devil.

Have you ever seen someone in the last stages of cancer? I have and it's an ugly, foul and evil sight. There is absolutely nothing good about it, nothing! It is an evil that destroys the person and families, wastes away the body, brings excruciating pain and misery and premature death. How could anyone possibly think that cancer can come from our Loving Heavenly Father?

Isn't it time for us to learn our part in continuing the work of Jesus in recognizing and destroying the evil works of the devil?

The thrill of victory, the agony of defeat

I feel at this point it is important to make something very clear. Although I pray for lots of people and see many people healed I also see people not healed. In fact in my own home group there are people who have chronic illness or disabilities. We currently have two meetings a week in our home and there is a good friend of mine who comes to both meetings. He has been crippled since he was a teenager and now he is in his 70s. He has probably been prayed for hundreds of times. Practically every time I see him, the fact that he is not healed yet hits me in the face. There is another dear friend in our group who has had migraine headaches for over 20 years.

I have known these people throughout all of my experiences in Tijuana, Veracruz, Barrio Logan, the jails etc. I have returned from various ministry trips and outreaches with a renewed faith for them because of my having seen the miraculous over and over again. But their conditions have not changed. I take my frustrations about their not being healed to the Lord often. He has really big shoulders. I have cried out for them and tried to find reasons why they are not yet healed. I sometimes get disillusioned, sad, very frustrated about them and others who don't get healed. I have wanted to quit praying many times.

But by the grace of God I have not quit. And by the grace of God I continue to be more and more committed to seeing more hurting people healed and free. I think of the hundreds of people I have seen healed and what might have happened to them if I had quit. So I refuse to quit. Even in the face of my 15 years of chronic headache pain I have continued to pursue healing for others and myself.

My own pain could have caused me to quit, yet deep down inside of me I was determined to continue to believe that my good Heavenly Father did not give me this pain. I continued to believe that God would make a way for me to be healed. In fact as I write this I have had relief of the chronic headache pain for the last year. It didn't come in the way I wanted, but believe me I'll take it.

Here is how it happened. The diagnosis by doctors of the root cause of my pain was a problem in my neck that was supposedly sending pain signals to my head. Well, it seems the doctors were wrong. One day I got a rash, a reaction to some pain medication I was taking and after calling my doctor she prescribed an allergy medication for it. After taking the medication for only a day or two I noticed that I didn't have any headaches. This continued day after day. And the final result is that a simple allergy medication is working to keep me pain free! My good Heavenly Father made a way! Now I am pursuing healing of allergies!

So, would you like my answer to why my friends are not healed and why I was not healed for 15 years? Here it is. Are you ready?

The answer is I don't know and I don't understand. And I have decided that I don't have to know the answer or to understand. I choose to believe that the problem probably lies down here rather than with God.

In the course of pursuing healing I have found that I can bang on Heavens doors for change in my condition and not give up in my pursuit of healing. But also, as Bill Johnson says I can decide to live "unoffended" at God. In other words, there's no reason I can't ask God for answers and not be satisfied with my condition, but I cannot afford to be angry at God when I don't get what I want.

Good news to the poor

Early in 2008 I was introduced to a homeless outreach, run by Hope Vineyard, in a local park in San Diego. This was where I met Mario, the man I told you about in the introduction to this book, who was dramatically healed. I started going there and was asked to preach and minister to the sick. Of course I decided to preach the good news of the Kingdom there. I remembered Jesus talking about preaching good news to the poor and I wanted to do the same. And I found, just as in the jails, that God has great compassion on the homeless, downtrodden and destitute. I found that my faith and the anointing of God increased when I was with these folks and more of the miraculous happened.

One night I was preaching the gospel of the Kingdom and telling people that they could get a lot more than just a hot meal. I told them that they could get their sins forgiven, eternal life and a relationship with God. I said God wanted their sickness healed and their oppression's lifted. I was telling them that Jesus was the same yesterday, today and forever and if that was true then He would come and people would be touched and healed and freed.

I declared the rulership and dominion of King Jesus, and that the Kingdom of God was at hand. Just as I have done several times before in previous outreaches, at a certain point in my message I asked how many people came with pain and how many people were now free of pain.

A gal named Rosie raised her hand and I asked her what her situation was. Rosie said that she had neck and shoulder pain because of beatings by her father for several years beginning at the age of 10. She was smiling and said that when I was telling about how Jesus wanted to show His love through His power she became free of pain! We were all overjoyed that this poor woman who was so abused, in pain for so many years and now homeless, had an encounter with the love of a Father who would help her and not abuse her. The heart and will of God as it is in Heaven came to Rosie.

Also a man named Mike who had a car accident in the early 80s was healed. He explained that because of the accident he had severe lower back pain for many years and therefore could not work (perhaps one of the reasons he was homeless?) We prayed for him two or three times and at the end he reported total healing and he said "now I can get a job."

After Mario and these others, I kind of thought it couldn't get better than this, but I was wrong. Remember how I said there is always more with God? Well, at this same homeless outreach I met a man named Bill Nicholson who, like Mario was walking with a cane. Bill was a man in his early 50s and although he was homeless he was clean, quite sober, and articulate. He wrecked his knee in 1972 after a fall from a high ladder. After a failed surgery the doctors could do no more for him. He had been in pain for 32 years and had to walk with a cane or crutch for all that time.

I remember praying for him three times over a ten minute period, each time I asked him to move his knee and take a short walk. After each prayer his pain declined from 7 to 4 to 2 to zero! When the pain got to zero I had him bend and walk a longer distance, still no pain. He gave his testimony to everyone there and threw away his cane in a trash can! I retrieved the cane and have it hanging in my living room to remind me of the goodness of God. It helps me especially at times when I am discouraged, experience disappointments or don't see things happen the way I'd like.

I arranged to meet Bill the next day and take him to lunch and I decided to get him a motel room for the night so he could get a hot shower and a warm and safe night's sleep. While we were eating a burger together he casually mentioned that he hadn't been able to see out of one eye since birth. I immediately got excited and told Bill that I would like to pray for him saying that if God healed his knee the night before why wouldn't God heal his eye? Bill agreed and stated that the most he had ever been able to see in his life had been an occasional dim shadow.

God had more for Bill

I had brought my video camera with me to record Bill's testimony about his knee. As we began to pray, I asked Bill to tell me about any improvement. After only a couple of minutes he started to see more distinct shadows. No objects at all just shadows. I started to get more excited and asked Bill if I could videotape what was happening because I felt that we were experiencing the beginning of a miracle.

So, here I was praying for Bill while holding the video camera. I continued to pray, commanding a spirit of blindness to leave and healing to come to his eye. My heart was pumping. I was saying to myself "could it be? Is this really happening?"

The shadows turned into blurry colored objects which turned into clearer and clearer objects. I of course had him cover his good eye as we prayed. My heart continued to pound and my hands were sweating as we both saw a miracle unfold in front of us! His sight continued to improve to the point where he was able to distinguish cars, buildings and trees and even read signs. At the end of our prayer time he had received about 90% restoration of the sight to his eye!

How happy do you think we were at the end of that prayer time?!

I checked Bill into the motel and followed up on him in the days ahead. His sight improved completely and he was now able to see clearly out of both eyes. Over the course of about two years Bill shared this wondrous testimony to the people at the homeless outreach. He has also come and shared it to a healing class I was teaching at my church.

We want to tell the world how wonderful Jesus is, don't we? What better way than a person like Bill sharing the miracle of having his sight restored? What better message can there be than relating a personal real-life experience of a here and now Jesus to other hurting people?

The big question

It should be obvious, but what was the will of God for Bill? Did God just decide at that moment that it would be a good idea for Bill to regain his sight or was it always in the heart of God that Bill would see? I would have never known until I decided to take the risk involved and pray in faith for Bill.

I would ask Bill and others who had been healed to share their testimonies as often as possible. Why? Because a person's testimony is powerful! When others hear it their faith rises and something inside of them says that if that person can be healed then maybe it can happen to them.

An example of this is Diane who I met at another meeting. After I shared the testimony of Mario's healing of curvature of the spine Diane came up to me and my wife for prayer. She had scoliosis, but she felt that the testimony I shared about Mario was meant for her and after prayer she reported her back being straightened also! Then she told us that she also felt free of chronic fear and anxiety which we hadn't prayed for! I love it when God does that! In talking to her a few weeks later she said she was doing great and came to our home group where I video recorded her testimony.

The power of the testimony

Did you know that the Ark of the Covenant was also called the Ark of the Testimony? The objects in the Ark, the stone tablets with the 10 Commandments on them, a golden jar of manna, and Aaron's rod that budded, were to be a testimony to the children of Israel down through the ages. Parents were to teach their children who were to teach their children about the great things that God had done. Why? God knew what the power of the testimony was all about. The Israelites were supposed to hear the testimonies of Gods deliverance from Egypt and provision in the wilderness. This was to help them believe and trust in God when they were in tough circumstances.

One of the root words for testimony means "do again." The testimony that Diane heard sparked something in her and she said if God could straighten Mario's back He could straighten her back. And He did!

We are told in the Scriptures to give God glory. I believe a good part of this means to talk a lot about the good things that God is doing. This is something else I have learned from the ministry of Pastor Bill Johnson. At the beginning of every meeting that he has with his staff they talk about the things that they have seen or heard of God doing in the recent past. And almost every time he gets up to preach he will tell testimonies about healings and miracles that he or his people had witnessed in the previous days and weeks.

This has become an important value at his church which has become one of the deepest wells of healing and the miraculous in the United States! He and I believe that this is substantially due to telling about the great things God is doing over and over again and building an expectation for God to do these great things again.

Freeing a captive

A friend was visiting from out of town. She was a kind and gentle Christian lady. During worship I noticed that she looked uncomfortable. I went over to her and asked what was wrong. She said she was feeling very fearful and anxious. I had seen the look on her face before and recognized it as a reaction to spiritual oppression. I asked her if she would like to go into my office for private prayer. She agreed, so I and a couple of my friends who knew her accompanied her.

Now, this lady was raised in a denominational church which did not believe in spiritual oppression in general and definitely not for Christians. But as I said, I had seen the look on her face before on other Christians who were spiritually oppressed. So, I pretty much knew how to proceed to help her.

Before I go on with the story I need to clear something up. We need to come to an understanding that not only do demons, devils or evil spirits exist but that they can oppress Christians. Many of us need to stop hiding our heads in the sand about this subject in order that we can substantially help hurting, oppressed people around us. Just because the subject is uncomfortable or controversial does not mean we should avoid it.

Over the last 100 years or so, much of the Western church has come to accept most demonic activity as mental or emotional problems to be dealt with by doctors. And, in the absence of effective prayer, doctors are a good resource. But, if we depend solely on doctors have we really arrived at a place of enlightenment? I think not in many cases. Jesus and the church down through the ages thought differently also.

Demonic oppression (or strongholds) is vastly different from demonic possession. In the case of possession a person completely loses control of some of their faculties. But, because the believer is filled with the Holy Spirit they cannot be possessed.

On the other hand, a demonic oppression or stronghold can take place when one or more areas of a normal healthy life are **strongly influenced** by demons. Through a variety of circumstances, such as unrepentant sin, unforgiveness, trauma, abuse, accidents, witchcraft, parental or ancestral sins or curses, a person, even a Christian, can be strongly influenced by demonic spirits. Things like sickness, addiction, fear, depression, anxiety or panic attacks are some of the things that can come from this type of oppression.

But, these are things which we are finding great success in relieving through prayer. There are many valuable books on the subject which will do the topic much more justice than I can right now.

But suffice to say, the lady who came to our home group was demonically oppressed.

When we took her into my office to pray for her we discovered that fear, anxiety, guilt, low self esteem and depression had been her companions for many years. That evening she was dramatically freed from some of those strongholds. And in the subsequent few days and weeks she was freed even more by others ministering to her. To try to tell her story in my words is difficult, but she sent me a letter a couple of months later sharing how grateful she was for our prayers and how free and alive she was feeling. She admitted that demonic oppression was never on her grid. She shared that things like that were not even talked about in her denomination, but she said there was no denying now what had taken place given the joy and freedom she was experiencing!

She gave me permission to give her name and I asked her to send me an e-mail outlining her experiences at our home.

Grace writes:
I grew up in a Denominational tradition and asked Jesus to come into my heart at age 7. I was told that now I had a relationship with God. I heard the gospel my whole life and believed it, but I knew nothing of the Holy Spirit and His presence in my life.

It seems like all I knew was rules and I learned a lot about judgment against all those that didn't keep the rules.... they were the carnal Christians. The overweight were gluttons. The rich were self-indulgent. I learned to judge and hate myself as well... I became anorexic late in high school...bulimia lasted until my 40s.

In college I met fellow students who had relationships with God like I have never seen in my life. They could hear His voice and knew His love!! I ached to have what they had, so I began a desperate striving in my flesh to obtain this relationship. All I knew how to do was to read my Bible and pray. So I was up at 5 AM every morning, on my knees in prayer. There wasn't an unmarked page in my bible.
Then I began to hear voices.... I didn't know what to do... with the voices came such oppression, a greater legalism and a lot of fear.

Once in a prayer meeting with my Spirit filled friends, the voices of fear were so strong I didn't know what to do. I see now that a demon was oppressing me, and with clenched fists and arms raised high I screamed out, "I've got to get out of here"! A brother grabbed my wrists and commanded the spirit to go. It left immediately, but I had no understanding of what had just taken place.

In 2003, the encounter at John's house happened. We were in his living room, guests at his home fellowship. We were worshiping and the passion to know more of God's presence consumed me. As I worshiped with my flute, suddenly everything went black. As I opened my eyes I saw John coming towards me smiling and asking what was wrong.

Then it happened. There was a violent wrenching of my body, and what seemed like angry tigers growling from somewhere within me or on me (?). The next thing I knew John and two of the people in his meeting were gently escorting me back to his office.

My body and head felt like it was wrenched like an old rag. Blood vessels burst in my eyes as I felt like my head was being squeezed. It felt like something used my throat to growl against John. But I will never forget the eyes of Jesus that I saw in John's eyes. He looked into my eyes with such compassion, asking if I was all right. Then with a fierceness and authority he commanded demonic spirits to release me. By this time I knew what was happening. I remember thinking, "I thought this only happened in Africa!"

I don't know how long it went on for, but finally my body and mind seemed quiet.

During this encounter I was taking authority over oppressive spirits who had tormented Grace for most of her life. This was a true "power encounter." At the end of our time with Grace she felt more peace and freedom from fear and voices than she ever had. The Kingdom of God had confronted the kingdom of satan and satan lost this battle.

Grace reported that there were other times during the next year that the power of other oppressive spirits had to be broken off of her life. This was done starting the day after she visited our house.

Grace continues:

More encounters took place five times during the next year... three times in church and twice at home. Each time, it was when truth was realized and spoken that the oppressive spirits had to go.

No, it's not just in Africa. I believe demonic strongholds in the West are very well camouflaged. Sometimes they can appear so nice and righteous. They keep things looking perfect, orderly and under control. And they can keep some of God's precious children in straitjackets; locked in performance and fear.

But I am free; I'm not a worm anymore. I'm His beautiful butterfly, His new creation. I am God's Grace. I'm His perfect one, the love of His life, the precious one for whom He died, I am beautiful, I am funny, I possess wonderful gifts and talents from my papa God, I'm His one and only, His darling. And I am free!!

He has transferred me from the kingdom of darkness to the Kingdom of His beloved Son. I know the truth and it is setting me free! This is the truth..... Jesus loves me! He really loves me!!

I love you John,
Grace

I know many people who are reading this story can only read it through their grid of teaching, tradition and experience. And because of that grid this story can seem bizarre, shocking and unbelievable. And that's all right. Exposure to this type of ministry and acceptance of it can take quite some time. But since you have gone this far in the book, why not be open to the possibility that some hurting people out there, Christian or not, could be dealing with circumstances like the one Grace described. Remember Steve? He did not have a grid for healing either.

The truth still sets us free

The Scriptures talk about knowing the truth which can set us free. How can we know we are being lied to or oppressed if we don't know the truth and what belongs to us as children of God? The enemy can get a foothold through lies leading to addictions, fear, anxiety attacks, depression, compulsive behaviors and a sense of self loathing or low self-esteem. All of which God wants to free His children from.

My advice for you is to read up on demonic oppression and talk to some mature believers who are experienced in this area. In addition I would investigate the books and teachings of Dr. Neil Anderson, founder of Freedom In Christ Ministries. His teachings show that believers can sometimes open themselves up to oppression by believing and acting on lies. Therefore he (and I) strongly recommend knowing the truth, especially about ourselves which can greatly help to protect us from oppression. The following are truths that need to become a very real part of the Christians thinking and believing. Another great read is Telling Yourself the Truth by Marie Chapian. Here are some scripture verses we all should own:

> **I am accepted**... John 1:12 I am God's child. John 15:15 As a disciple, I am a friend of Jesus Christ. Romans 5:1 I have been justified. 1 Corinthians 6:17 I am united with the Lord, and I am one with Him in spirit. 1 Corinthians 6:19-20 I have been bought with a price and I belong to God. 1 Corinthians 12:27 I am a member of Christ's body. Ephesians 1:3-8 I have been chosen by God and adopted as His child. Colossians 1:13-14 I have been redeemed and forgiven of all my sins. Colossians 2:9-10 I am complete in Christ. Hebrews 4:14-16 I have direct access to the throne of grace through Jesus Christ.
> **I am secure**... Romans 8:1-2 I am free from condemnation. Romans 8:28 I am assured that God works for my good in all circumstances. Romans 8:31-39 I am free from any condemnation brought against me and I cannot be separated from the love of God. 2 Corinthians 1:21-22 I have been established anointed and sealed by God. Colossians 3:1-4 I am hidden with Christ in God. Philippians 1:6 I am confident that God will complete the good work He started in me. Philippians 3:20 I am a citizen of Heaven. 2 Timothy 1:7 I have not been given a spirit of fear but of power, love and a sound mind. 1 John 5:18 I am born of God and the evil one cannot touch me.
>
> **I am significant**... John 15:5 I am a branch of Jesus Christ, the true vine, and a channel of His life. John 15:16 I have been chosen and appointed to bear fruit. 1 Corinthians 3:16 I am God's temple. 2 Corinthians 5:17-21 I am a minister of reconciliation for God. Ephesians 2:6 I am seated with Jesus Christ in the Heavenly realm. Ephesians 2:10 I am God's workmanship. Ephesians 3:12 I may approach God with freedom and confidence. Philippians 4:13 I can do all things through Christ, who strengthens me.

What is our mission?

I strongly believe that Jesus' mission is our mission. His mission was clearly stated by Him in Luke chapter 4 verses 16 through 19. This is how it reads:

He went to Nazareth, where He had been brought up, and on the Sabbath day He went into the synagogue, as was His custom. And He stood up to read. The scroll of the prophet Isaiah was handed to Him. Unrolling it **He found the place** where it is written: "the Spirit of the Lord is on Me, because He has anointed Me to preach good news to the poor. He has sent Me to **proclaim freedom for the prisoners and recovery of sight to the blind, to release the oppressed, to proclaim the year of the Lord's favor.** (Emphasis mine)

What is compelling to me about this passage is that first of all Jesus unrolled the scroll of the prophet Isaiah. The book of Isaiah is over 100 pages long in my Bible. I don't know how many feet long it would have been in His day. But, it says He **found** this particular place to read. I believe He **intentionally went looking** for this passage in order to make a very strong statement about His mission and the purpose of His coming into the world. Freedom to prisoners and release to oppressed captives is a main part of this passage. I believe that proclaiming freedom for prisoners and release to the oppressed includes demonic oppression and possession as well as healing the sick.

This mission of Jesus was continued when we, in the power and authority of the name of Jesus freed our friend Grace from her oppressive captivity.

It is quite obvious that Jesus did not free the Jews from political oppression or captivity but from spiritual oppression, captivity and bondage. Yes, He came to free and heal "all who were oppressed of the devil." (Acts 10:38)

Although we should neither obsess on the demonic nor dismiss it, there is great need for this type of ministry in and outside of the church.

A spirit-based affliction

I don't know about you, but there are just too many people in the world around me who are in serious need of freedom from oppression. Let me give you another example. James was another friend who came to our home group meetings; he had chronic pain, cramping, numbness and tingling in his legs and hands and general weakness in his body for a long time. We prayed for him three times and each time the pain disappeared for one to three days and then returned. The third time we prayed, all the pain and discomfort again left and it occurred to me that this was probably a spirit based affliction. So, after we prayed and we came against a spirit of affliction all pain once again left. **I instructed James to take up his part in his healing and to rebuke/resist/say no to a spirit of affliction and pain if it tried to return.** It did try to come back but James said no to it a few times, standing firm in his faith and that Jesus had healed him. He has been free of pain ever since (almost 2 years).

This is a very specific case of physical infirmity directly caused by a spirit. The Bible says in James 4 "submit yourselves to God, resist satan and he must flee from you." This is a perfect example of healing someone of a physical problem who was oppressed by a spirit and the person having to resist the spirit. I seriously doubt it was the devil in person because he cannot be everywhere at once, but I am sure it was one of his demons. James has also received significant freedom from fear and anxiety attacks as we and he prayed along these lines and as he took responsibility to resist fear and tell himself the truth. He, too, had no grid for what was taking place in his life. He hadn't had much teaching, if any, about spiritual oppression. But now he knew first hand. It's amazing to me how an experience with God can trump a neat and comfortable traditional theology or no theology.

Resist and say no first

Did you ever consider how much effort is needed to remove something that has been there for a long time? In my friend James' case he had a long-standing affliction which took a bit of effort to get rid of. We had to pray three times and then James had to resist the spirit of affliction that brought the sickness.

I believe God wants to bring His children from a place having sickness, to a place of being healed of sickness, to a place of staying in health. One of the ways of doing this is by taking good care of our bodies. Another way is to resist the very first symptoms of pain and sickness in our bodies.

Now this may be a real stretch in the thinking of some people. But, I have applied the principle of resisting symptoms of sickness at the very beginning, when they first appear. Why? Because, in the many years that I have been used by God in healing the sick, I have come to a very basic conclusion. My belief is that God would rather have us well and whole rather than sick. Because Jesus healed everyone who came to Him sickness is something to be fought against.

Paul said that we have an adversary, the devil, who roams around seeking whom he may devour. Paul says WE should resist him firm in the faith.

If Jesus didn't like sickness, I don't like sickness. If Jesus didn't like oppression, I don't like oppression. If Jesus came to destroy the works of the devil and went about doing so by healing the sick, then He must have viewed sickness as not a part of God's will for people.

So, if I view sickness the same way, then I should resist it when it tries to come my way. I do this by believing that symptoms of pain and sickness and disease that try to attach itself to my body are alien invaders. It's as if someone came to my door with a package with the label marked "Symptoms of Sickness and Disease inside." **I have decided not to sign for the package!** I refuse to sign for any package I don't think Jesus is sending.

And I have to say that my approach has been very successful although not perfect. Applying the principle of resisting the works of the devil that try to attach themselves to my life is an ongoing process which I am getting better and better at. Just in the past six months I have encountered many symptoms in my body, some of which have been alarming. I have resisted them all in the name of Jesus and I can honestly say that not one of them has led to any long-standing sickness or pain.

I plan on continuing to decline acceptance of the packages that the enemy tries to send to me! How about you? (See page 182 about how resisting and believing has worked to finally get me free of headaches).

Another miracle in the park

On another night at the homeless outreach, the Kingdom of God advanced once again. I prayed for Bobby, a homeless man, whom I saw limping severely and using an old golf club for a cane. He limped right in front of me and took a seat right next to me. My heart went out to him. I introduced myself and asked him what the problem was. He told me that he had torn his hamstring and had been walking around in pain for several weeks. He also showed me his right foot which was turned out almost at a 90° angle from his left foot. He also said that one leg was about an inch shorter than the other. So his limping was due to several reasons.

It just so happened that Bobby sat right next to Bill Nicholson, the man who was healed of a 32 year knee injury and who got sight back in an eye that was blind since birth. I told you Bill's story in a previous chapter. I told Bobby about Bill being healed a couple of years ago at this homeless outreach. Bill concurred and told Bobby a bit about his miraculous healings, (the testimony).

When I offered to pray for Bobby he quickly agreed. I prayed for his hamstring and commanded healing and freedom from pain. I then took Bobby's arm and helped him off his seat. As soon as he stood up an amazed look came over his face and he shouted "I don't believe it"! He began to stomp his bad leg and jump up and down. It looked like he was trying to do a tap dance! I think he shouted again. This caused a bit of a commotion at the outreach because it happened during a time of worship.

Question....is God allowed to interrupt a worship service so that one of these children can get set free? Remember Jesus in the synagogue?

I sat Bobby down and began to pray for his turned out foot and his short leg. I held both of his feet in my hands to see the difference in length. What I didn't notice was that his turned out foot had already turned inward and as soon as I began to pray the first words of a prayer for the legs to come to the same length, they evened out right in front of our eyes! He again got up shouted, danced and leaped! I felt like I was back in the book of Acts! And why not, God wants the book of Acts to continue doesn't He?

The very important story behind the story

God wants to heal not only physical but emotional wounds. Jesus mission included healing the broken hearted and complete redemption.

Bobby shared that he was a follower of Jesus but he had really struggled with his faith. As a matter of fact Bobby had a drinking problem and had been in and out of jail even though he was a believer. He felt that he had totally disappointed the Lord and God had no more use for him. I got the sense that he thought that God was punishing him. I said to him, "If God was punishing you Bobby, why would He heal your legs?" A look of understanding and agreement came over his face.

That night God showed him His steadfast love, mercy, and compassion. Whereas Bobby thought that God was through with him and punishing him; God reaffirmed His love and commitment to Bobby by healing him. What was the will of our loving God in Heaven for Bobby? Healing and restoration! I believe that this may well be a turning point in Bobby's life. This power encounter with the here and now loving Savior will help get Bobby tracking again with Jesus

In fact, about a week later, Larry Johnson, a long time friend who helps run a Christian drug rehab called me. He said I had something that belongs to someone he knew. When I asked what it was he told me it was the golf club that Bobby had used as a cane.

He was joking of course because Bobby gave me the golf club after he was healed at the homeless outreach. He then went back to the drug rehab to apologize and try to get reinstated. After hearing about his miraculous healing, Larry did just that, saying that he saw a significant change in Bobby's demeanor, attributing it to the miracle.

A hurting world is waiting for us to take our place as true sons of God, and take the risks necessary to advance the Kingdom and will of God as it is in Heaven, for people just like Bobby. Decide to start now and take a small risk of faith today! As you start to take small steps of faith, your faith will grow and a loving here and now Jesus will become more real to you and the people you pray for.

Yes, your personal faith can be enough

There is a place in the New Testament Gospels where a Centurion comes to Jesus about a servant of his who was at home and paralyzed. Jesus was about to go to the Centurion's home to heal the servant but got a better idea from the Centurion. The Centurion believed that Jesus didn't have to go physically and that all He had to do was say the word. It's incredible to me that the Centurion's faith actually changed the mind and method of healing of Jesus, the Messiah, the Son of God! That was a major point of the story for me.

Here's the reason. Jesus always respects the faith and belief of others. Over and over again we see Him saying "your faith has healed you or be it done unto you according to what you have believed." A secondary point was that a long distance miracle took place, showing us that there is no distance in the spiritual realm. We can pray for people from any distance just as if they were standing right in front of us.

Ernie, the miracle magnet

Ernie is an example of a long-distance miracle. Ernie is a friend of Alin James, one of the co-leaders in our House Church. Ernie had been plagued with several bouts of cancer in various parts of his body for about 10 years. Over this period of time he had cancer of the colon that required surgery, radiation treatments for prostate cancer, and was diagnosed with bone cancer and carcinoma of the bladder. It seemed like Ernie was a cancer magnet.

His battle with cancer continued and our group began to pray for him even though he had not yet attended a meeting with us. We told Ernie that we were praying for him and expected God to heal him. This is what he wrote to me:

> A very dear friend and work associate, Alin James, recommended that I attend a prayer group meeting that he was associated with that believed in healing by the power of Jesus Christ. This was a Christian group that had prayed and experienced miracles of the Lord that had happened for people over the years.
>
> I decided to see for myself if this was indeed happening. You could label me as the "show me type" before I would believe. After several meetings, I started to believe in Christianity and its healing powers through the Lord Jesus Christ, our Savior. Miracles began to happen to me and have continued since. Some of the miracles that have happened to me are as follows:
>
> During my last bladder surgery all pathology reports showed that I no longer had cancer in my bladder. (No detection of any cancer cells).

My most recent bone scan showed that there was no longer any cancer that was detected in my bones. This was something that doctors were amazed at. No radiation or chemotherapy had ever been done to me.

I was diagnosed with kidney and liver cancers. I had a tumor removed from my kidney and it was malignant per the pathology reports. After more prayer they did a second exploratory surgery, it was determined to be all clean of cancer! All the liver tests were also redone only to find that everything was back to normal PRAISE THE LORD!

I fell and broke 4 ribs at my daughter's house. This was verified by my primary care doctor by x-ray. While in bed at my home suffering with a lot of pain, the prayer group called and prayed for me over the speaker phone. Within one hour all of my pain was about gone and I had no pain or indications that I ever broke my ribs the next day!

All of the above miracles of God have happened since the death of my wife of 39 years. On three different occasions doctors have given me one to two years at most to live. Thanks to the Lord I am still here and feel wonderful!

God has also done many miracles of restoration within my family. My gratitude goes out to Jesus Christ, my Lord and Savior along with all of the people who have prayed for me for my good health, my being saved by the Lord and all of the joy and happiness that has been given to me.

From the most recent doctor's pathology report available, Ernie is now cancer free!

On the night after Ernie tripped and broke four ribs, I heard he was in excruciating pain and taking medications that were causing nausea. My immediate response was that I began to talk to my wife about how painful it was going to be for Ernie in dealing with four broken ribs and how long it would take for him to heal. A couple of minutes into this dialogue I caught myself and said "**no**", we need to pray for Ernie tonight and go after healing for him."

I was heading down the road of natural thinking. But, I am learning to take that first thought captive and replace it with the truth. What was the truth? It was that broken ribs are just another thing that God wants to heal. Broken ribs are something that Jesus would have healed and another thing that is not part of the will of God in Heaven. I'm glad I changed my mind. And, so is Ernie.

That night, our group prayed for him over the speakerphone. Ernie began to move and touch his side in expectation of something happening.

In my mind I was saying "oh no, he's pressing his broken ribs." Having had rib injuries in the past, I was imagining just how painful that would be. This was just another challenge to my thinking and faith. But Ernie was reporting that he was feeling less and less pain. In about five minutes he was about 80 to 90% free of pain and his nausea had completely decreased to the point where he said he was going to make himself something to eat! The next day he was pain free! After this we started calling Ernie a "miracle magnet." But in reality it was simply the will of God done for Ernie. **So, why shouldn't we become miracle magnets, expecting God to do the miraculous on our behalf?**

The important point to this story is that I could have continued in natural thinking about Ernie's ribs. After all, according to natural thinking broken ribs should have remained painful and taken quite some time to heal. But according to the will of God as it is in Heaven, healing Ernie's ribs was just one more good thing that our good God wanted to do.

We all must learn to continually go back to what God's viewpoint is, and what Jesus would have done in a similar situation. I just can't see Jesus saying, "Sorry Ernie, broken ribs are a little too tough to handle" or "it's not your day for a healing."

It is not easy to change our thinking, because we all have been living in natural thinking for many, many years. We will remain so until we begin to receive teaching, modeling and mentoring in the area of faith and seeing from God's viewpoint.

But why waste time? Let's start now. Let's look at each situation and try to determine the will of God in it. And then pray **and believe** accordingly.

The disciples get it

In Luke 9:1 it says, "Then He called His twelve disciples together and gave them power and authority over all demons, and to cure diseases. He sent them to preach the Kingdom of God and to heal the sick."

I can just see the disciples going into a town and asking this question, "Is there anyone here sick or demonized?" I can see them being led from house to house driving out demons and healing the sick. I think it was after people had seen these miracles that they inquired as to how the disciples could do these things. I also think it was a simple gospel message of the Kingdom at that point..... "The sick in your town have been healed because of Jesus of Nazareth would you like to know him." "The demonized in your town have been set free because of Jesus of Nazareth would you like to believe in him?"

10

"...the equipping of the saints for the work of service."

Rodrigo and I worked together in the mid-90s. During that time my wife and I would drive to our local church and pass a group of somewhat run down apartments. It's seemed that every time we passed them I would feel a slight tug toward the people in these buildings. The tug wasn't much but it was there. I started to get the feeling that I should get involved with the people there. I got the sense that there was something that God wanted to accomplish in those apartments.

I was holding a series of outreaches to teenagers at the local Salvation Army campus and Rodrigo came to several of our meetings. Rodrigo was hungry for God and willing to make himself available. At one point he asked me, "John, how can I help you in your ministry?" When he asked me that, I immediately thought of the apartments. I asked him if he was willing to move in to those apartments and begin reaching out to the families and especially the youth who were so vulnerable to gangs and drugs in that area. A single man at the time, Rodrigo agreed and for the next three years he did incredible work reaching out to these families. He established soccer teams for the kids and Bible studies for all. Many came to the Lord during those days. Many lives were changed and redirected because of his willingness to make a difference. I am so grateful to him for making himself available to the Lord.

The years passed and Rodrigo got married, had kids, and became a pastor of a small church. In 2008 he asked me to come to his church to do some healing, equipping and training meetings. He said his people were quite open to what I was teaching and they had a desire to learn how to co-labor with God in healings and the miraculous.

Their faith would dramatically increase over the course of three Sunday meetings, because once again God showed up big time. When there is an atmosphere of faith and acceptance of healing and the miraculous many more cool things can happen.

On the first Sunday I arrived and preached the Gospel of the Kingdom. I told them that Jesus was the same yesterday, today, and forever, that not only **could** He heal but that He **would** heal and free people in their church and that they could learn to be used by God to do the same. Once again God showed Himself to be powerfully present. Here is a rundown of what took place in his church:

Jennifer was healed of pain in her legs after I shared the testimony of the woman at the Barrio Logan outreach and her knees being healed. Jennifer was simply sitting in the meeting listening to me give testimonies of other people's healing. No one prayed for her or laid hands on her. This was another example of the power of the testimony.

Sam was a bass player in the worship band and his finger was injured and his knee was in pain. He reported both were healed.

Adela was healed of a two month shoulder injury; a big smile came on her face as she moved her shoulder without pain.

Fernando was suffering from severe acne sores all over his face. He was hesitant to get prayer or even step up to the front of the room because of the embarrassment of how he looked. Over the course of three weeks his face completely healed. He became like a new person because of this healing. He was no longer ashamed and had a new confidence!

The ugly face of demonic oppression

José is a man who had a history of epilepsy and epileptic seizures. He would have these seizures regularly, several times a month. The doctors of course had diagnosed this as a neurological disorder and tried to control it with medication without much success.

But, this was to be an example to José and the church, of demonic oppression resulting in the disease of epilepsy.

When I laid hands on him and began to pray he dropped to the floor like a sack of potatoes. I had seen this before and started to pray against a spirit of epilepsy commanding it to release him from its oppression. Although I spoke directly and strongly to this spirit in the name of Jesus, I did not raise my voice. Loudness does not constitute authority.

The people around us were a bit frightened but I assured them that I had seen this before and that God was setting him free. José seemed to lose consciousness, but after only a few minutes he got up from the floor and reported that he was feeling free and lighter and believed that he was healed.

On a subsequent visit, about a year later, I asked him how he was doing and he reported that he was free of epileptic fits for almost a year. Then he said about a week before I visited for the second time he had an epileptic fit. I prayed for him once again then instructed him, as I did James, to resist that familiar spirit of epilepsy in the name of Jesus and I have heard that he has been free ever since!

Can you imagine the terrible stress and desperation that this ugly demonic disease brought on José and his family? I wonder how many times José might have asked why God gave him this. But now everyone was seeing the joy that he had. They realized that not only did God **not** give him this, but God **delighted** to take it away!

More fun stuff

Edith had a back injury and pain for quite a long time. I remember the big smile that came to her face when all the pain left her and she reported her back was healed.

Esmeralda had four years of pain and aching muscles. She reported being completely free after prayer.

Arecelli reported freedom from 15 years of migraines headache pain after we rebuked a spirit of affliction and infirmity! On my return visit a year later she was still free.

Ignacio reported being free of pain in his teeth and an injury in his toes.

Beto reported being completely freed of 14 years of pain in his foot on the first Sunday I was there. By the next Sunday he said that about 25% of the pain had returned. After again coming against a spirit of affliction and pain I instructed him on resisting and he reported being free from then on.

Pastor Rodrigo had back pain. When we began to pray for him the pain moved from his back to his stomach. Then it moved again. I had seen this before recognizing it as an oppressive spirit which moved when it was addressed by authority. We commanded the spirit to stop its oppression; to release him and Rodrigo reported being freed of pain. With a little more prayer he also said he felt free from a sense of oppression, heaviness and guilt! God is such a full-service Father!

Everybody gets to play

During one of the meetings I got some of the people who were healed involved in praying for others, just as I had done in Veracruz. I asked those who wanted to pray to come and form one line and those who wanted prayer to come and form another. Many of the people doing the praying had never prayed for healing before. I matched them up. Out of about eight people being prayed for, six reported being healed immediately. I did this again the following week, so that people could be more confident that God would use them. And of course He did. More people reported being healed or free from oppression.

When people buy into the premise that God **wants** to heal and do miracles, and also that God wants to use them, lots of great things happen. In an atmosphere like that, when the pastor is hungry and willing to take risks and when he encourages his congregation to press into these areas, faith, healings and miracles flow much more easily. Pastor Rodrigo led his church into an entirely new realm of power, faith and confidence in themselves and God. I've heard reports of some of his people taking their experiences and the love and power of God to their family and friends, and to the streets and the marketplace around their church! It seems the risks that pastor Rodrigo took were worth the results. I am very grateful to him that he trusted me to equip his people.

God corrects me and assigns us

The church Fran and I attend is called Journey Community Church in La Mesa, California. It is a 2500 member evangelical, friendly, come as you are church. It has a warm, welcoming and relaxed atmosphere and the leadership is hungry for God. The lead pastor, Ed Noble, has an incredible teaching gift, functioning in the office of a teacher and has a deep hunger for more of God. I look forward to his gift being released every Sunday. There are three services a weekend and at every service there is an invitation given for people to become followers of Jesus. Many take the offer.

Fran and I first attended this church several years ago when our son was serving on the worship team as a musician. It was Easter Sunday morning and we went there to support him in his service to the church. We were definitely not looking for a church to attend at the time since we were pastoring a home church meeting weekly at our house. In fact we didn't really like large evangelical churches to be honest. And to be more honest I was somewhat judgmental in my heart about them. Our preference was for smaller, more intimate type churches. So, on this Sunday morning I figured we would just visit and say hi to our son, Chris, and go on our way.

God had other plans.

When Jason, the worship leader, began to play the first song, I felt the familiar warm and wonderful presence of the Holy Spirit come over me. I started to tremble slightly and tears flowed out of my eyes. I was enveloped in warm love and the sensation stayed with me through most of the worship service. I had experienced this before at times when the Lord just wanted to bless me with His presence, and at other times when He wanted to communicate something to me. I was asking the Lord what was going on. I felt the Lord's say on the inside of me, "I'm here John."

I love the Lords brevity and pinpoint accuracy when He speaks. Because, when He said that, I knew exactly what He meant. He was convicting my heart because I really didn't think He was there. Oh, I knew He was there theologically, but I didn't think He was there in the power of the Holy Spirit. In His wonderful grace and mercy He gave me an experience of His Holy Spirit and gently corrected me. Well, I want you to know I repented immediately. I said to the Lord "it's obvious that You are here and I am sorry that I misjudged this church." It has taken me a long time to learn this and God has been very patient with me, but I now refuse to judge **any** other Christian church. I try hard not to say negative things about them and their congregations

In the weeks ahead the Lord showed us clearly that He wanted us there. It is so much fun to be clearly and powerfully led by the Holy Spirit. So, as led, we kept going back and in a couple of months joined the prayer team. We felt we were to support the leadership in their hunger and quest for more of God. Since that time I have had the privilege of being allowed to teach a couple of healing classes, and on a weekly basis, as part of the healing team, we are encouraged and excited about the things that God has for this church and what He is doing there! The following are just a few of the things that have happened at the hands of the prayer team and others at this church.

Although I don't know complete details I must share three of the most dramatic and powerful healings that have recently taken place.

I heard the report of a woman who was literally on her deathbed in the hospital. The doctors had given up any hope at all and advised the family to say their goodbyes. After being prayed for by some members of the church both in person and from afar, she was completely healed and she returned to church in just a couple of weeks!

We just heard the report of a woman who was diagnosed with breast cancer. After prayer the doctors discovered that the cancer was completely gone!

Several of us on the prayer team prayed for a woman who had back pain from an accident eight years prior. She had a pain level of 7 to 8. After prayer for her we asked her to slowly move and bend and tell us what her pain level was. She was reluctant to do this because of the pain.

But, slowly and hesitantly she bent over and then a big smile came across her face as the pain left. She started to cry and laugh at the same time!

A group from our church went to visit a man in ICU at Sharp Memorial Hospital. He was in a bicycle accident, had a severe head injury and was unconscious when we got there. The reports from the doctors were not good. We prayed for him, left and the next day he regained consciousness and has since completely recovered and is back to work to the amazement of his doctors.

I usually ask people with pain to try to pinpoint the level of pain on a scale of 1 to 10. I do this because I expect some immediate results and I like to evaluate progress and build on the slightest improvement. So, if a person's pain level is eight and it only goes down to six or seven I begin to celebrate the improvement and encourage the person to begin to get happy and thank the Lord for this sign of progress. Then we will pray more and usually the pain level will decrease even further and sometimes completely disappear.

I look at it this way; I should expect some kind of results every time I pray or why pray at all. On most occasions where Jesus and the disciples prayed the answer came quickly. The goal I am reaching for is the model I see in the Gospels. So, if I expect healing why shouldn't I investigate to see if healing has begun? Many times a person will get slight improvement and then our combined faith can rise at that moment to go for more. In short, I look for both total healing and any improvement whatsoever and continue to pray.

I have tried to make it a point to pray for every person at least three times. Jesus had to pray for a blind man twice. If I don't see anything happen right there and then after I have prayed, I choose to encourage them to believe and I choose to believe. I encourage them to continue to get prayer and I always choose to walk away believing that God has heard us and has begun the process of answering our prayers.

More at Journey...

Another woman came for prayer for a friend. After praying for the friend I asked her if she had any health problems that we could pray for. She said yes that she had lower back pain. I felt led to just place a hand on her shoulder and not pray out loud at all. I told her this and after a minute or two asked her what the Lord was doing. She said she was experiencing heat, perspiration and tingling going from her head down her back to the place where the pain was. She was shaking and could not stand.

We got her a chair, continued praying and she reported that she received major relief and an incredible spiritual and emotional encounter with the Lord's love and His presence. I love it when God gives people more than what they asked for. In this case she was not even there for herself, yet God gave her freedom from her own affliction and a wonderful experience with Himself.

A similar example was a woman who came for prayer for family problems. We prayed for that and then I asked her about her own health. She said, "Oh, my back has been hurting for years." I got the feeling that she was resigned to just living with it. So, I pressed in a little and shared with her that God could heal her back also. We prayed and her back suddenly straightened surprising both of us and she reported being free of pain. She neglected to tell us at the beginning that her back pain was the result of scoliosis. Her back had straightened right in front of our eyes!

A woman reported being freed of asthma and back pain which went from a level 5 to 1. Through tears of joy she also reported that the sense of depression and anxiety was gone!

Another woman asked for prayer for her heart, she also gave forgiveness during this time. There was pain in her back which she had not mentioned but after the forgiveness her back pain went from 9 to 0. Again tears of joy!

A young man came up for prayer for an addiction to pornography. He said he didn't know how to get free, but I told him that if he renounced pornography and we prayed together, he could be free. He repented; renounced pornography and we both came against a spirit of pornographic addiction. Several weeks later he came back saying that he had been freed.

Even more...

We prayed for a woman who had been suffering from depression and been on meds for some time. After leaving her in a prayer of forgiveness towards others, we took authority over the affliction and over any demonic spirit of depression and fear and she reported that she felt an immediate lifting and lightening. I suggested she remember how we resisted the spirit of depression and fear and encouraged her to do the same if the symptoms tried to return.

A couple that various team members have prayed for had suffered a series of miscarriages. Here is an e-mail report from that woman:

We want to share with you that our baby boy was born on May 1, 2010 at 4:39 AM. He weighed 7 pounds, 13 ounces, and was 21.5 inches long...we rejoice in God's faithfulness and blessings. We can't thank you enough for the prayer support we received from you and from the prayer ministry over the past months.

I prayed for a young man who was diagnosed with clinical depression and was suffering from fear and anxiety. This is what he e-mailed me:

> I wanted to take the time to let you know how much better Jesus, with your prayers, made me feel today! I feel like I have been delivered from some major bondage that was really, truly sucking the life out of me! I feel like there is hope for me again. I don't want to ever lose this feeling I have right now. I feel at peace and my head is at rest. I am so happy and have hope. I love it. I love Jesus. And I love what you did for me. I don't want to go back ever again to that darkness.

At our church we have a monthly time of extended worship and prayer which we call SELAH. Our pastor Ed Noble heads this up and here is what he reported by e-mail about one of these meetings:

> It always feels a little risky heading to Selah. We honestly don't know what exactly is going to happen. We are there to worship, to pray and to see what God might want to do. We deliberately have a minimal agenda. We also want to make space to respond to the Lord's movement.

> There were several stories of God at work. Here's one: We were in the midst of a prayer time. There was a line of people waiting to receive prayer with our prayer team. So, as I'm just enjoying the worship, out of nowhere, my lower back starts hurting. I didn't think a thing of it, but then the thought came to me, "Is this God speaking to me." It seemed as if it just might be, so I said in the microphone, "If you have lower back issues, I think there's grace for you." That night I got this on Facebook:

> Hey – I ALREADY have a testimony from tonight – The past 2 Sun's I have LITERALLY been sick to my stomach because of **lower back pain**. I went up for prayer tonight and felt IMMEDIATE relief. Got in my car – sat down and twisted – my back cracked in such a way that I could move and SOOOOO much stress just evaporated out of my body. God, WOW!!! What a night – I just thank EVERYONE that was there tonight PULLING on God so that I and so many others might be healed and have HOPE!!!! LOVE YA!

I held 2 classes at our church. The title of the classes was "Healing the

Whole Person." The reason for this title was that I believe that the church, the body of Christ, is called to bring God's wholeness to people in spirit and soul and body. The class had several purposes. The first was to share my experiences and my discovery of God's willingness to use someone as ordinary as me. The second was to teach about the Kingdom and what was included in it. And the third was to make it an equipping and empowering class to help people step into the arena of being used by God.

I decided I would challenge people right away, so I put two things on the whiteboard. The first was the word "all." In the first class I talked about how Jesus healed all who came to Him, how that was the will of His Father then, and that the will of His Father had not changed today. I said that the goal of the class was to go towards "all." And, that if we don't get to this goal in our lifetime it's okay as long as we maintain steadfastness in working towards it. This word "all" caused a bit of a stir and I was glad that it did because it made people think and challenge what they had believed for so long.

Because, we the church, are not used to all being healed, we assume it is not the will of God to heal all, or at least many, many more than are receiving healing. I think one of the reasons for this is that many believers have let their experiences and disappointments override the truth. I tried to explain that although we don't see all being healed right now, it is still **the will of God as portrayed by the life, words and works of Jesus.** I explained that believers need some credible standard to determine the will of God. Jesus words and works were the revealed will of His/our Father and that will of His/our Father has not changed. What has changed is the thinking, teaching, traditions and theology of the church in an effort to explain why all do not get healed.

The second thing I put on the board was "fully conformed into the image of Christ." As previously mentioned in this book this means allowing God to conform us not only into Jesus' image of the compassionate, kind, loving and merciful Son of God **but, also into the image of the healing, freeing, and miracle working Jesus**.

An example I used for this is Peter, who asks the Lord's permission to come to Him walking on the water. Most of us would be okay if Jesus had said "Now Peter, you know that walking on water is reserved for me only. Peter, you are being prideful and arrogant thinking that you can do what I did." But Jesus didn't say that, did He? There was no rebuke, no disdain and no shutting down of Peter's desire to walk on water. He said joyfully, "Come on Pete."

My own picture of this scene is Jesus beaming in a broad smile because Peter was "getting it," and simply wanted to walk on water like Jesus. Peter was getting the idea that Jesus wanted His followers to be like Him **in every way.** And even when Peter succumbed to fear Jesus didn't let him sink. I believe Jesus was glad that Peter tried and helped him by telling him how he could have succeeded. The lesson for Peter and the lesson for us is that Peter could have walked all night on the water with Jesus if he did not succumb to the fear and doubt presented by the storms wind and waves. I can't count the number of times I have let fear and doubt stop me from taking the risks that God wanted me to take. But I don't plan to remain this way, do you?

Another example is when the 5000 were hungry and Jesus said to his disciples "you feed them." I believe He meant for them to actually do the creative miracle themselves by multiplying the fish and the bread. But, although they didn't get it, He helped them learn the lesson and worked with them to do the miracle. He had them participate in the miracle as the food multiplied first in His hands and **then in their hands.**

The point I was trying to make in this very first class was that Jesus wanted Peter, His disciples, and us fully conformed into His image; the image of the healer, deliverer of the oppressed, raiser of the dead and the miracle worker. Isn't it sad that many of us believe that it is too radical a belief for us today? Conformed into a compassionate and loving person, fine, conformed into a healer and miracle worker, no way. That was just for Jesus.

You see, to a large extent I have proved this out in the years before I presented these classes. I had to get over a lot of erroneous teaching, traditional yet wrong thinking and my own disappointments. I am at a point where God is continually challenging me to believe that the impossible can be changed and be changed by God through me.

Throughout the classes I tried to model Jesus' rabbinical teaching style. I **taught** how God wanted to use them just the way He had used the early church disciples. I gave them chapter and verse about the Kingdom of God, power and authority and the mission of the early church being the same mission today. Then I gave them a prayer model to work with, **demonstrating** how I and others prayed for people, and how God could use them in different ways as they were led by the Holy Spirit. **Then I had them pray for others while I overlooked and advised** and then **I let them pray on their own.** I hope I did the rabbinical model justice.

One of the most important things I tried to get across is that failure is part of the process of succeeding. We see the disciples getting it wrong over and over again. I gave the members of the class permission to try and fail and stated emphatically that doing it wrong is part of getting it right.

Many cool things happened during the class "workshop times" when we had people actively praying for one another.

At the end of the final class I handed out a survey for the class to fill out. The results of the survey indicated that people indeed did feel empowered to step into the area of healing and the miraculous. And some of the reports of what took place were very encouraging.

A missionary who attended said he was personally strengthened to overcome doubt and have confidence to pray for the sick as he returned to the mission field in China.

Some of the reports of healing were as follows:

A woman reported that her shortness of breath was healed and she experienced freedom of pain and discomfort in a wrist and hand. This same lady also reported that she had experienced "a wonderful feeling of peace when class members laid hands on me and prayed about my anxiety. Now my anxiety levels are much lower."

Another gal shared that she "received healing from depression, fear and anxiety." She also reported being healed from neck problems and an infection.

I felt that the class empowered people and gave them a new perception about God's desire to do the miraculous and to do it through ordinary people. Some of the folks subsequently joined the prayer team. And some who were already on the prayer team reported coming away with more of a sense of confidence in who they were and their part in God's healing plan for people.

And then there was Steve, the man I spoke about in chapter 5, who was taught that healing wasn't for today. God healed his shoulder anyway and Steve said "this has changed my mind about healing and now I want to give it away to others."

Part Two

The story of Jesus and the
early church can be your story.
My story can be your story.
I pray that your story far exceeds mine.

If this book ended here you would have some great stories of God's miracle working power in someone else's life. But, if you want to be the person God uses, you will have to do a little work. The following chapters, **if absorbed and acted on** can launch you on your own adventures in the power of God. You can have the joy of seeing many hurting people healed and set free! It's not a big leap; it's simply a matter of taking the first small steps.

11

My top 12 core values and foundational truths regarding healing and miracles

Since my days in Tijuana in 2000 I have tried to be aware of the things that motivate me, keep me moving forward and give me faith and confidence that God wants to continue to use me. As I move through life these days, I find that I **must** recall these things at different times and in different circumstances.

1. **The loving will of God has been revealed in Jesus.**
He said, **"I only do what I see My Father doing... if you've seen Me you have seen the Father and... I and the Father are one."** The loving will of God was clearly displayed and demonstrated in the life, words and works of Jesus. We cannot make presumptions about the will of God that go against what Jesus said and did. We cannot build a theology from our experience which says God doesn't want or is reluctant to heal or do miracles today, as freely as when Jesus walked the earth.

God is love! God heals because love heals. God doesn't do evil. Love doesn't do evil, but does good. ("Which of you being evil know how to give good gifts to your children?") Jesus "went about doing **good** and healing **all** who were oppressed of the devil."

Jesus is the exact expression of God's will. Jesus is the will of God demonstrated. If you want to see God at work, look at Jesus; if you want to hear God talk, listen to Jesus. When Jesus healed the multitudes we see the Father revealing His will. We see God at work.

A pastor that I highly respect said that he read a report by some theologians of the Episcopal Church. This was years ago. After an appointed commission spent three years of study and research in the Bible and history the report concluded:

> The healing of the sick by Jesus was done as a revelation of God's will for man. No longer should the church pray for the sick with faith destroying qualification, "if it be thy will."

Bill Johnson likes to say: "We have good news, about a good God, who is in a good mood!"

If it was the loving will of God that Jesus heal everyone who came to him then, it is still the will of God today. Why would that change? (Some people make the ridiculous claim that because we have the Bible we don't need healings and miracles today. How absurd! I only need to look around me to see how much we need healing and the miraculous.)

It is not recorded that Jesus turned anyone away, at any time, for any reason. He simply loved them too much to do that! I must decide once and for all whether this was a demonstration of the Father's loving will or not.

What has to change are my conclusions which are based on my experiences or faulty teaching. I believe that when we begin to change our thinking, our conclusions and our faulty doctrines, this will result in seeing many more people **healed and saved.**

I try to say to myself, "I know God wants to heal this person because Jesus would heal this person", and then I ask God how He desires to do it. Every time I pray, I expect the person standing in front of me to be healed or set free then and there or that the healing process would begin at that time.

About power and authority

I choose to believe and remind myself that Jesus passed His power and authority to His followers down through the ages and finally to us. I usually don't ask God to heal people. The reason is that He has sent **us** to heal in and through the power of Jesus, His Spirit in us and in His name. When He sent the 12 and the 70 out He said, "Heal the sick." The assumption is that they would take authority and power over sickness in His name and do as they were told. Why should I ask God to do something that He has already given me the authority to do in and through His name and His resident power in me? It would be like a policeman who sees a robbery in progress and calls the chief of police to ask him to come and arrest the robber. If he did that I'm sure the chief would say, "What are you calling me for, you've gone through police training, you're on my force, you have the gun, the badge and the backing of the entire police force, I placed you out there so carry out your job."

2. God still uses ordinary, imperfect followers of Christ to accomplish healings and miracles.

I am one of them. So are you! Jesus chose 12 guys who were ordinary and imperfect followers. Later they would become extraordinary, imperfect followers.

Judas betrayed the Lord. Peter denied Him three times. Others sent mom in to get them a seat at His right hand, others wanted to call fire down from Heaven and destroy a whole bunch of people, most fled at the arrest of Jesus, others debated about which of them were the greatest. They failed a lot. They gave up. They didn't "get" who Jesus was and wanted Jesus to set up His Kingdom right away and appoint them as members of His cabinet!

Yet Jesus **chose and sent** these men. But if these were the only ones that Jesus sent out we might assume they were especially enabled or anointed "Apostles." But Jesus sent out 72 other ordinary and imperfect people, to do the same works as He and the 12. There is very little in the gospel record that tells about these other 72. They were not part of the in-group or the specially anointed 12 apostles. Yet Jesus sent them out. Healing, miracles and gifts of the Spirit continued. Then there were the miracles at the hands of Stephen. Healing and miracles and gifts of the Spirit followed Cornelius in Acts 10:44, Ananias in 9:10-18, Agabus in 11:28 and 21:10 and the prophets Judas and Silas in 15:32.

The epistles tell about other non-apostles who experienced the supernatural and gifting. Paul tells the Corinthians that none of the gifts is missing among them and Peter says that each one has received a spiritual gift in 1 Peter 4:10. Prophecy was used in Rome and Thessalonica (see Romans 12:6 and 1 Thessalonians 5:20).

And then Jesus opened it up to you and me today by saying "**Anyone** who believes in Me, the works that I do shall he do..." Yes, He meant the same works that He did and we the church are his **anyones** and are His plan to change the world around us. God's plan **is** His people. In fact weakness and imperfection are good characteristics for those who want to be used by God. Paul recognized his weaknesses and said, "**....** **But we have this treasure in jars of clay to show that this all surpassing power is from God and not from us.**" The fact that we are ordinary pots of clay, in which He chooses to put Himself, only results in Him getting the glory He deserves. Sometimes I marvel that God uses a cracked-pot such as me to do incredible things. He will do the same for you. Anyones and cracked-pots are pre-qualified and invited!

3. **God is conforming me fully into the image of Christ.**

If I were to say this in many of our churches today most church people would say, "Amen, yes, I agree God wants to conform me into the image of Christ." But, many sincere and committed Christians believe this is **only** to the extent of conforming them into Jesus' love, kindness, compassion, mercy, meekness and humility. Very worthy desires, but, why should I stop short of being **fully conformed**...into His power and authority over the demonic, sickness and disease? There is no question that Jesus wanted His ministry and mission to continue at the hands of His followers. Would He leave us without power and authority to do this?

But, I also believe, along with many respected, recognized, and credible teachers and theologians that the empowering of the Holy Spirit is necessary to fully and powerfully carry on His mission.

John the Baptist said that Jesus would baptize, (flood or immerse) us with or in the Holy Spirit and that we would receive power at that time.

In the beginning of the book of acts Jesus **commands** His disciples to wait for the promise of the Father and that they would be baptized (flooded or immersed) with the Holy Spirit, so that His followers would receive power to be all that Jesus commissioned and commanded them to be. Now, Jesus had previously breathed on them to receive the Holy Spirit, but now, He is saying that they needed more, they needed this baptism, this flooding, this immersion, and this encounter with the very person of the Holy Spirit.

I say we need all the help we can get, why not do life with all the means available that Jesus wants us to have. If He said we needed to be flooded or immersed in the Holy Spirit in order to serve him fully and powerfully, then that is what I want.

4. **The Kingdom of God is here and now**.

The rulership, authority, dominion and power of the King are some of the essential ingredients of a kingdom. King Jesus brought the Kingdom and demonstrated what it looks like on earth and He gave it to me/us ("it is the Father's good pleasure to give you the Kingdom"). The Kingdom not only offers forgiveness of sins and eternal life through Him, but healing, freedom from demonic oppression, and abundance of life. We must remember that Jesus sent His disciples out to heal the sick, raise the dead, cleanse the lepers, cast out demons, and declare that "the Kingdom of God is at hand." The very acts of healing the sick, raising the dead, cleansing the lepers and casting out demons **demonstrates that the Kingdom of God is here and now. Jesus wanted an on-going Kingdom and an on-going rulership and dominion to take place over the works of the devil**. Which works...all the works that Jesus took dominion over.

5. The credentials of Jesus the Messiah were not and should not be only in words.

Which credentials can we, the church, present to the world? When John the Baptist sent to Jesus and asked, "Are you the one or should we look for someone else?" Jesus' response then should be the same response of the church today, but it's not. When asked this question Jesus didn't go into all the Scriptures and prophecies about Him coming into the world. He didn't talk about the things He said about Himself or what others said about Him. He sent back to John a different response outlining the healings and miracles which were done at His hand. He said, "Go back and report to John what you hear and see: the blind receive sight, the lame walk, those who have leprosy are cured, the deaf hear, the dead are raised, and the good news is preached to the poor...."

I believe with all my heart that Jesus still wants this to be the response to people who want to know if Jesus is real and who we says He is. And why not? Jesus said, "If you do not believe Me for the words that I say, believe in Me for the works themselves..." Shouldn't the credentials of Jesus be the same today? Shouldn't the credentials of Christianity be the same?

Although God doesn't have to prove anything to anybody, Jesus chose to point to the healings and miracles as the "proof" of who He was. There are many people in the world who are adhering to philosophies, theologies and religions which are based on words. And they do good charitable works. We need to have a faith based on more than words and good charitable works. Otherwise we will be just another good religion. There is only one that is based on a here and now disease healing, miracle working, demon destroying, life giving Jesus! I strive to learn to give the world **this** Jesus as well as a sin forgiving, eternal life giving Jesus.

6. Jesus came to destroy the works of the devil and I am to continue His mission.

He demonstrated this by healing the sick, cleansing the lepers, raising the dead and driving out demons. These were some of the **works of the devil** that Jesus came to destroy.

Although God can and does use any circumstance and can turn it around for our good, even the works of the devil, God does not send debilitating, body wasting, life killing, disease, pain and affliction to teach us something, humble us, build our character, or draw us closer to Himself. He is a bit cleverer than that and He has much more loving and kind ways to do those things.

I come across people who've been sick for many years and believe that God sent the sickness on them to teach them something. But most usually find out that they haven't learned much except how to be

125

miserable, depressed, defeated and hopeless. God cannot be a very good teacher, doing it this way.

To those who say "This must be my thorn in the flesh," I say "When did you go to the third heaven and have incredible revelations that cannot even be spoken?" Paul's thorn was a "messenger of satan." Why do we attribute it as a messenger from God? If it was a messenger from God I think the Scripture would say that. Also, to assume that the thorn was sickness is more of a stretch then to assume it was the Judaizers who dogged his heels constantly beating him and throwing him in jail. Paul was a "died in the wool" scholar and Old Testament teacher. Whenever the phrase "thorn in the flesh" was used in the Old Testament it meant problems with or from people. It was used as we would use the phrase "this person is a **pain in the neck**," or another appropriate area of the anatomy. I bet Paul used in the same way.

Why is it that we choose a few scriptures to override all the overwhelming proofs that it is the will of God to heal as seen in the life, words and works of Jesus? It's almost as if we want to believe that God kind of, sort of, wants us sick rather than well. God forgive us of this way of believing.

7. **Jesus, the 12, the 70 and people like Paul, Stephen, Philip and others all preached the Gospel of the Kingdom.**

This included salvation, forgiveness of sins, eternal life, a new beginning, and healing, deliverance, signs and wonders. Why should the gospel I preach be anything less? Paul wanted the new believers at Corinth to have a faith that was rooted **in power** and not just in words! Jesus said, "If you don't believe Me for the words I say believe Me for the works themselves..." I aspire to the goal of being able to say the same thing to the world around me. Although I may not see the fullness of this goal attained in my lifetime, I must reach for it. Why settle for less? I must continue to offer hurting people not only forgiveness of sins and eternal life through Jesus Christ but also healing and deliverance which was included in the gospel that Jesus preached. Anything less is not the gospel that Jesus and the early church preached and demonstrated. This is the gospel that will usher in the return of Jesus. "**This** Gospel of the Kingdom shall be preached in the entire world as a witness and then the end shall come."

8. **"As it is in Heaven" is the will of God today.**

Jesus taught us to pray "Your kingdom come your will be done on earth as it is in Heaven." Why would Jesus give us this prayer to pray if He didn't fully intend that it be answered in the here and now as well as in the millennium? This has been a prayer for every generation throughout the last 2000 years, and it was meant to be a prayer for a current reality for each generation. "Your Kingdom come (now), Your will be done (now) (just as) it is in Heaven." I believe this is as much a declaration as it is a prayer.

Some relegate this to a future time only. Yet the future is now. The future is the time between Jesus coming and Jesus returning.

Jesus brought His Kingdom with Him and demonstrated "the will of God as it is in Heaven" all the time! Because it was not the will of God in Heaven, sickness had to go. Because it was not the will of God in Heaven, demonic oppression and dominion had to go. Because there was no leprosy in Heaven, the lepers had to be cleansed! Jesus demonstrated the will of God, and sent out His disciples and us to bring "the will of God as it is in Heaven" to hurting people.

Bill Johnson has some powerful things to say about "Your Kingdom come, Your will be done on earth as it is in Heaven." On page 60 of his book "When Heaven Invades Earth" he says:

This is the primary focus of all prayer. If it exists in Heaven, it is to be loosed on earth. It's the praying Christian who looses Heaven's expression here. When the believer prays according to the revealed will of God, faith is specific and focused. Faith grabs hold of that reality. Enduring faith doesn't let go. Such an invasion causes the circumstances here to line up with Heaven. The critics of this view sarcastically say, so, I guess we're supposed to pray for street of gold. No!

I don't believe he is saying that everything that is now in Heaven is supposed to be here now. I do believe he is saying that the will of God as it is in Heaven **and as demonstrated in the life of Jesus** should be the rule now.

We should be striving to bring at least as much Heaven to earth as Jesus did. He didn't bring streets of gold, but He did bring life and life abundant to all the hurting people He healed and set free. And why would this happen? Because that was the loving will of His Father in Heaven, and He only did what His Father in Heaven was doing. Whenever I pray for someone I try to think of whether or not their need is something provided for by the will of God as it is in Heaven or demonstrated by Jesus. I can then go ahead with confidence.

When I pray for someone I will sometimes **declare** the rule, reign and dominion of God over them. I will say something like:

I declare the Kingdom of God over you, I declare the rule and dominion of God and His Kingdom over every part of your spirit soul and body. God rules over you. Let the will of God as it is in Heaven take place now! Will of God be done in you just as it is in Heaven! Any demonic oppression is now subject to Christ in me and the power of the Kingdom of God. Any demonically inspired sickness, disease, pain or suffering must yield to the Kingdom of God and the Lordship of Jesus Christ now!

9. After prayer for someone, I must walk away believing.

I love it when people are instantly healed or set free right in front of my eyes and it happens more now than ever. I usually pray for someone at least three times in a prayer session looking for the slightest bit of improvement as well as an amazing miraculous solution there and then. But, when nothing outwardly happens, I must make a choice. I must choose to believe for this person.

Believing is a **choice and a decision** and not a feeling. It is based on the will and character of God as demonstrated in the life and works and words of Jesus. It is not based on what I or the person I am praying for feel or see. The person I pray for needs and is worthy of my faith. It is good if people have their own faith to be healed, but, even if the person we pray for has zero faith we can have faith for them.

Lazarus and his family had no faith that he would be raised from the dead. It wasn't even on their radar. But Jesus had the faith. I have chosen to believe until. Until what? Until when? Until something happens. I owe it to people I pray for to believe with them and for them! And I try to encourage them in their own faith by pointing to the healings and miracles of Jesus and giving them testimonies of people I know who have been healed of the same or similar things they have.

10. Testimonies glorify God and increase faith for the miraculous.

The Bible from cover to cover is full of testimonies about what God has done for people. The Ark of the Covenant was also called the Ark of the Testimony. God wants to continue what was started back then. He wants the accounts of His greatness to be handed down from generation to generation. But more than that, He wants them to be handed down and talked about in our everyday lives When we give an account of what God has done, it says "God can and will do that again." It builds the faith of those who hear and it gives them hope that if God will do it for one, He will do it for them.

Many times, when a person comes for prayer I will tell them about someone else who was healed of the very thing they are struggling with. In fact I tell most people who come for prayer for any reason that I have seen God give sight to a man who was blind in one eye since birth and give hearing to a boy who was deaf since birth. I try to bring the person to a place of saying to themselves "If God can do that for another, He can do it for me too!"

In more than one meeting I've held, people have been healed of the same or similar problems as the testimony I had been giving and without anyone praying or laying hands on them! It is reason enough to give testimonies because God is glorified in the testimony. It is honoring to Him and a form of praise and worship.

11. I must not disqualify myself from praying for healing or others from being healed.

I am qualified to heal the sick by virtue of being included in the words of Jesus when He said, "Anyone who believes in Me, the works that I do shall he do and greater works..." if Jesus includes me as a qualified "anyone" then I must include myself.

I can disqualify myself every time I say I don't have enough faith or I am not trained or smart or educated, or holy enough. Every time I go to pray for someone I find that I **must** remind myself that I am righteous and holy in the sight of my Father by virtue of what Jesus did for me on the cross and not by virtue of my good works.

It is good to pray and study the Bible and seek the Lord on a daily basis and I try to do that. But if I don't do it on a particular morning I am still qualified and worthy and usable to God. You see, the one who is the same yesterday, today, and forever is with me, in me and for me and for the person I am praying for.

Also, I must not disqualify the person I am praying for. Since Jesus didn't disqualify anyone from being healed I cannot do that either. I have to set aside what I may know is lacking in a person's life, otherwise I may put myself in a place of judgment. I wrote earlier about a prison inmate whose arm was numb from the elbow down because of drug use. God did not disqualify him from being healed because he was a criminal or a drug addict.

12. Jesus didn't pray for the sick.

What! That sounds far-fetched but in reality we don't see Jesus praying to the Father that the Father would heal the sick person.

It's true. He knew the will of the Father in Heaven and by power and authority He executed that will on earth. The Father had given Him a mission, to release captives and prisoners, to heal the sick, raise the dead and cast out demons and in that way bring the Kingdom of God to bear and destroy the works of the devil. Therefore with confidence He did that, and we can exercise the power and authority to do the same by virtue of the same mission.

His mission was to become our mission, that's why it was part of the great co-mission. Just like a police officer, or soldier, we have been recruited and trained to exercise power and authority in this world on behalf of God and for the benefit of hurting humanity. But, let's try to do it the way Jesus and the early church did. When He sent them out He said "heal the sick" not pray that I or My Father will heal the sick. He said" drive out demons" not pray that I or My Father will drive them out. Of course we do it all in and through the name of the Lord Jesus one.

Exposing the strongman

In Matthew 12: 22-29 and Luke 11: 14-26, Jesus gives us good insights into spiritual warfare, dealing with the demonic and binding the strongman or the strong spirits who come against God's people. Since Jesus associated the demonic with many sicknesses we need to give it close attention.

Please see page 175 for more on this very important subject.

12

Will the real you please stand up?

"If the devil can't get you to sin big then he will make you ineffective by telling you how weak, small, unholy and unworthy you are." I have made this statement for many years and believe it very strongly. How can we possibly be effective in the Kingdom if we think that we are not much better than an unworthy worm?

All throughout Scripture we see God encouraging people to step into the image of how He sees them. We must begin to view ourselves as God views us or we may live a very ineffective life. We must see ourselves as carriers and brokers of a very powerful Kingdom and ambassadors of a very powerful King.

It is not prideful to say what God says about you in the scriptures. Jesus didn't think it was prideful to call Himself the Son of God and the one who was to come into the world. Why? Because it was the truth. We need to apply God's truth to our view of who we are. So begin to **read and meditate on these verses and actually believe them & say them to yourself and others**! When we know the truth about ourselves, the truth **will** make us free and freer to be used by God.

> **Matthew 5:3-14...I** am the **light** of the world and the **salt** of the earth. I am called to be and bring light to those in darkness and be a preservative of all that is good! There are so many people around us in darkness but our light can show them the way out.

Romans 4:22-25, 5:1....I am **righteous** before God by faith in Christ and have peace with God.

Our enemy accuses us all the time of being unworthy and unrighteous. But, as Jesus did in the desert, we must use the word of God to refute the enemy. I am the righteousness of God, therefore I am worthy to be used by God to do the works that Jesus did.

Romans 8:11....The **same Spirit** who raised Jesus from the dead lives in me. When I pray for people I release and see myself releasing the powerful Spirit of God to them through my hands and words! This amazingly powerful Spirit of God can take care of any problem. He lives in us, but He wants out, to be released to others!

2Cor 5:20-21....I am an **Ambassador** of Christ and His Kingdom. As His Ambassador I **fully represent** His government, power and the authority of His Kingdom. I broker His desires everywhere I go and toward everyone I speak or minister to! I bring the rulership and dominion of the Kingdom of God to bear in the lives of hurting and oppressed people.

Eph 1:1-14....I am blessed with **every** spiritual blessing, **chosen** in Christ, **holy and blameless** before Him, **forgiven**, have an **inheritance** and I am **sealed with the Holy Spirit** who guarantees my inheritance. WOW! Chosen, holy and blameless certainly qualifies us to be used powerfully and give His love away to many! This is the real me, not the lowly worm that the devil wants me to believe I am.

Eph 2:4-6....I am **greatly loved** by God, made alive with Christ and **seated with Him** in Heavenly places (I can minister with Christ **from** that position of being seated with Him). As I meditate on my true spiritual position as being seated with Him I then can begin to minister and **pray from Heaven to earth**. From that position I am the head and not the tail. From that position I am superior to and have authority over demonic forces. I can minister from a place of absolute power since I am seated with Him now in that place of absolute power. It is ministry from Heaven towards earth and not the other way around. I am not trying to get something from Heaven I am releasing something from Heaven because I am seated with Him in Heaven.

Col 1:27....Christ, the hope of glory, **dwells** in me. Christ in me is powerful and I release Him to others in need.

Col 2: 9-10....**All the fullness of the Godhead dwells in Christ**, And, if all the fullness of the Godhead dwells in Christ, and Christ is in me, then all the fullness of the Godhead dwells in me also.

Heb 13:8....." Jesus Christ is the same yesterday, today, and forever." Therefore all the works that Jesus did when He was on the earth He is still doing through His body, the church (you).

1 Peter 2:9...."But you are a **chosen** generation, a **royal** priesthood, a **holy** nation, His own **special people**...!" I am holy and royal and chosen... how special we are, how chosen, how royal, how holy! This should give us confidence as we minister to others.

The importance of receiving and giving forgiveness

I am a forgiven forgiver. In order to enter the Kingdom we must know we are freely forgiven and just as important we must choose to freely forgive.

Do you keep rehashing the past, remembering sins and mistakes over and over again? This is the place your enemy would like to keep you, in the guilt and shame of the past. It is very difficult to move forward or feel good about yourself when you keep living in the past. Our enemy wants to keep us in the past with shame, guilt and regret or in the future with fear and anxiety. Jesus talked about the present being the place to stay.

Either the past is dead and all your past sins and mistakes are under the blood and forgiveness of Jesus or they are not. It's time to decide. Have you received cleansing and forgiveness once and for all? If not, do it right now.

The long lists of do's and don'ts are not to guide us as they did in the days of the Old Testament. We are now to be guided by the Holy Spirit and by the words that God writes on our hearts. If we are looking at our lives under a magnifying glass to find out whether we are living right before God we put ourselves under the Old Testament Law which Jesus came to fulfill.

A friend of mine, Pastor Ken Blue, used to depict the law like this: "the law is like the policeman who pulls behind you while you are driving. He puts his lights on and motions you to pull to the curb. You know he's not pulling you over to tell you how well you are driving, how nicely you are keeping the speed limit, or how beautiful a right hand turn you just made. No, he's pulling you over to lay it in to you for doing something wrong. So, it is with the law, it never has anything good to say to you."

So we must choose: Do we want to live under law or under grace and the leading of the Holy Spirit?

Sins and mistakes need to be admitted to God and forgiveness needs to be received by us on a constant basis. Then we must go forward as if we had never sinned. Since God remembers our sins no more so should we.

Just as important as receiving forgiveness is the ongoing process of forgiving others. In much of my 30 + years as a follower of Jesus, I have come across perhaps the most important factor relating to sickness, a life of peace, and keeping ourselves from giving satan strongholds in our lives. That is unforgiveness.

Unforgiveness can become a stronghold which has at its roots unrepentant anger, resentment, bitterness, hatred or desire for revenge toward others.

Perhaps as many as 70% of people I have prayed with for a variety of problems including serious sickness and disease, have had to deal with unforgiveness. In leading them towards the decision to forgive I usually ask them if they like the forgiveness that Jesus has given to them. I will emphasize how wonderful it is that Jesus forgave them all of their sins and continues to do so on a daily basis. I share that if He, who had been severely mutilated by His enemies and hung on a cross, could choose to forgive His tormentors and then us, then we can forgive also.

I go on to stress the fact that forgiveness is a command of Jesus (Matt 6:12-15). I also stress that it is a choice and decision and usually is not accompanied by warm fuzzy feelings for the person that hurt them. Those feelings may or may not come later yet our decision to forgive **must** take place. Forgiveness does not deny the fact that the person hurt, abused, or terribly wronged us. And forgiveness doesn't mean we let a person back into our lives if they are a habitual abuser. Sometimes for chronic abusers it is best to forgive them from a distance and stay away from them. Abuse that could be criminal should actually be reported to the authorities yet forgiveness still needs to be given.

Someone once said, "Unforgiveness and harboring resentment, bitterness, etc. is like drinking poison, hoping that the other person will die."

The magnitude of unforgiveness is so clearly illustrated in Matt 6:12-15 that we should make forgiveness an everyday part of life.

Yes, we have been forgiven the day we received Christ, but subsequent and ongoing forgiveness must take place.

13

Praying for people

According to your level of desire to be used by God in the areas outlined in this book, God will use you. As mentioned before, you have been pre-qualified to be used. But, only as you seek the Lord and take small and then larger and larger risks, will you see more things happen. What do I mean by this?

At the very beginning of my journey in these areas I went to the Lord and said that I really desired to see the miraculous as it was in the days of Jesus and the early church. I "pressed into" the Lord a bit in this. And then I decided to step out and take the risks involved. I really didn't have any formal training. But I decided to try and take the risk of failure. Do that and you're on your way.

In actuality, as far as training is concerned, by having read this book you are pretty much as trained as I was when I first began. You see, God was more interested in me simply wanting to do these things and making myself available to Him, than in my ability and training.

My quick start program

In the pages ahead I will go into much more detail about steps, procedures and methods. They will be helpful, but they are not essential for you before starting.

If your church has a "prayer team" who actively pray for people with the laying on of hands then join their team and read the books I have recommended in the bibliography. Most of what I am outlining in this chapter can be applied to that type of prayer environment.

And, since we all live in the age of the "easy button," here's my quick start program which can be applicable anywhere and anytime. You can start immediately and be trained as you go.

1. **Pray and go**.

Go to the Lord, spend time soaking in His presence and then talk to Him about being used to pray for hurting people around you. Tell Him that you believe that He wants to use you and that you will have your antenna up so He can show you people in need. Write down any feedback you may hear from Him. From my experience, He will encourage you in this because it is His will and His heart. Intimacy with the Lord is essential to being used by God. In intimacy we fill up on Him to spill out to others.

2. **Be available to hurting people.**

Keep your antenna tuned to the heart of God for people around you who are in need. Press through fear of failure and rejection and open up conversations with people in a friendly, casual manner and ask about their situation. Try to feel what they're going through. Perhaps you can relate their situation to a past situation in your life when you needed help. Offer to help by praying for their need right there and then. Tell them that God cares about them and their situation and wants to help them. You will find most people are happy to talk about their situations and happy that you offered to pray. Smile, don't be intense. As you do more of this it will get easier. If they should decline, tell them that you will pray for them on your own later. If someone should say no, don't take it personal. Of course this is easier in a church setting when people are coming to you as a member of the prayer team.

2. **Pray for them.**

Get permission to put a hand on their shoulder and pray quietly, but out loud, from your heart. I have found that God will back up the simplest prayer for people. It doesn't have to be a perfect or eloquent prayer. Begin to **speak to** the problems by a prayer of command in the name of Jesus. I.e. shoulder be healed, pain go, bone be mended, spirit of death and cancer be gone, spirits of sickness, disease, infirmity, affliction leave now in the name of Jesus Christ of Nazareth etc. Ask God to bless them and give them peace.

3. **Get feedback**.

If time permits, ask them how they were doing during the prayer and if they are feeling any better. You might offer more prayer at this time. If you are feeling a connection you might want to invite them to know Jesus, visit your church or connect with you by e-mail.

If you can join a prayer team at your church, do so and ask to be paired up with a more experienced person. The church atmosphere is an ideal and safe place where you can learn. A friend of mine said that the meeting place is the training place for the marketplace. So, starting in the church is a good first step.

It really can be as simple as that. But, in order to go deeper and get more fully equipped I strongly urge you to get John Wimber's book "Power Healing" and if you can afford it, "Power Evangelism." I recommend reading the books, taking some notes and then go back to the parts that point out specific things you feel God is showing you to learn. For me these are the best primers on healing I have read. And I will try to integrate important parts of John Wimber's detailed healing model here, quoting many passages.

From pages 99 through 134 of "Power Healing." He writes:

I developed a procedure through trial and error that I call "five steps to healing prayer." Each element of the five steps is based on Jesus' method of praying for the sick, though in Scripture these steps are not presented in a systematic and chronological fashion. So, the application of Scriptural truth, not merely the pattern of my personal experience is the basis for this method.

I want to add here that the Lord spoke directly to John Wimber at a point early on in his ministry. It's important for us to take these words for ourselves...the Lord said to him **"preach My Word and not your experiences."** We must hold fast to the truth of God's Word and what He says about things regardless of our past experiences, especially in the area of healing and the miraculous.

John continues:
Each of the five steps attempts to answer a question about the sick person's condition: what is the condition? What is its cause? How should I pray for it? When should I stop praying? What should the person do to stay healed? These steps are quite practical and simple to follow. In only one conference session most people can learn enough to start praying for the sick immediately. In other words, this method helps people to know where to start and when to stop in praying for the sick.

This five-step model may be used anytime and anyplace: in hotels, at neighbor's homes, on airplanes, at the office, and of course, in church settings. I have been in casual conversations with people, even with complete strangers, who mention some physical condition and I asked, "May I pray for you?" Rarely do they decline my offer to pray for healing, even if they are not Christians. I then confidently pray for them by following the five-step method.

The five steps are:

Step one: the interview
Step two: the diagnostic decision
Step three: the prayer selection
Step four: the prayer engagement
Step five: Post prayer directions

Step one: the interview

The interview answers the question, "what is the problem, where does it hurt?" I ask what do you want me to pray for? Then I listen to the answer on two levels the natural and the supernatural. The natural level evaluates the answer in light of my biblical knowledge, what I know about the person, and my past experience in praying for similar problems in other people. This is not a medical interview in which we probe for technical, medical history. A (detailed) medical history is important for medical treatments, but not for praying for a person's healing. The Holy Spirit is the doctor and the cure; He does not need our technical knowledge to heal. Besides, detailed medical discussions usually only delay healing prayer."

I personally like to ask these questions: " what would you like Jesus to do for you today or if Jesus was standing in front of you right now what would you ask him for?"

I want to add here that during the interview we want to get to the problem fairly quickly. A brief history of the problem is fine but the more we allow people to go into extreme details and an account of how specifically bad the problem is, we can find ourselves succumbing to unbelief. What happens is that the problem and the symptoms begin to get bigger and take on more of a reality then the power of God.

Step two: the diagnostic decision

....this is identifying and clarifying the root of the person's problem. The diagnostic decision answers the question why does this person have this condition? This is a crucial step in the healing procedure because it determines the type of prayer needed to bring healing; in fact, this procedure overlaps with the first step. While I am interviewing the person, on a supernatural level I am asking God for insight into the ultimate cause of the condition. These insights usually come to me through words of knowledge, words of wisdom, and distinguishing of spirits. (See 1Cor. 12:1-11) Only infrequently do people know **the true root** of their problem.

For example, two years ago Kevin Springer prayed for a woman who had severe back pain. During the interview the woman said that her injury was caused by a physical mishap several years before. But from her response Kevin suspected that something other than physical damage was the source of her back pain. After a short and fruitless time of prayer, the woman returned to her seat, discouraged because her back still hurt and this was yet another failed attempt at divine healing for her.

As she turned, Kevin received a specific insight from the Lord into her back problem: that it was related to a poor relationship with her mother. This came to him as a thought: "Her mother. There is a problem between her and her mother." Because of this insight, he called her back for further prayer.

When the woman returned, Kevin asked her if she was having problems relating to her mother. He said, "Even though you said that you had injured your back in an accident, I believe the Lord is saying that somehow your back problem is also related to a problem you are having with your mother. What do you think about that?" She confirmed problems that went back to her childhood, though at first she did not make the connection between her back and her mother. At that point Kevin decided that in fact that healing of the woman's back was related to the healing of her relationship with her mother and that inner healing was needed before physical healing could happen. After helping her extend forgiveness to her mother and to receive forgiveness for her sin, Kevin began prayed for her back. This time she was healed instantly. A year later she wrote Kevin to confirm that her back remained healed.

As I mentioned before many roots of sickness can be in unforgiveness. Don't be afraid to approach people with this root of sickness, especially if they want to be free of the condition. Most people are willing to forgive when it is simply pointed out as a possible route to the healing of their sickness. Keep in mind forgiveness is a choice and decision **we can make** in light of the forgiveness we have freely received from Jesus

John continues:

Root causes may be quite complex as this story illustrates. Symptoms in one area of our lives may be caused by problems in several other areas. The following examples illustrate the complex interrelationships among the physical, spiritual, emotional, and social parts of our lives.

Once I was asked to pray for a woman with arthritis. I asked her, "How is your marriage?" She answered, "I am estranged from my husband. Three years ago he left me with six children." I said, "Well, there is a possibility that your feelings about all of that had been buried in resentment and bitterness and that is what is causing this condition. How do you feel about that?" She said, "I don't think so." So I said, well let's just pray about that and see what God does, okay?

As I began to pray the Holy Spirit came on the woman and penetrated to the deepest part of her heart. She was able to see her bitterness and resentment towards her husband. She forgave him and then received healing prayer for her arthritis. She said she was healed. Several months later she confirmed that she remained healed. In this instant physical sickness was caused by harboring resentment.

I have also prayed for men and women who are unable to sustain healthy relationships because they have been hurt by a marriage partner. They are incapable of receiving or giving love, even with fellow Christians. This is an example of social problems caused by emotional hurt that came from sin, sin either by them or against them.

I frequently encounter demonic oppression that causes fear and as a result creates emotional problems that result in physical problems.

An example of this was a woman whose fear, caused by a demon, made her insecure with her husband, which contributed to her problem of feeling like a failure as a wife. These factors in turn caused barrenness. Once the demon was cast out of her life, she was able to love her husband more freely and conceive a child. In this instant an emotional problem was caused by demonic influence and resulted in a physical problem.

I have found sometimes that doctors words or the negative words of family or friends can become a type of a curse over us. If we completely buy into the diagnosis and the resulting suffering and misery that could be in the future without holding on to our God, for whom nothing is impossible, then the diagnosis can be a prophetic word of doom. Similarly, family or friends can say things to us which can actually take root and cause problems such as sickness or other negative emotional problems. We must continually go back to the Jesus, who turned around impossibilities, and receive His diagnosis that nothing is impossible with God. We also must go back to the truth about who we are in Christ and who He is with and for us.

John continues:
When I first described the range of causes for illnesses (the list is almost limitless), most people think they are unable to discern these causes. They look at me and say, "It's easy for you. Look at all your experience. It has taken you years to learn how to understand these things." I admit that I have grown in my ability to diagnose these problems over the years, but I have grown mostly in sensitivity to the Holy Spirit's leading and insights, not an academic understanding of human psychology or medicine. This is not to imply that growing in psychological or medical understanding works against divine healing. The Holy Spirit is the one who leads us through the diagnostic step. He walks with us, accompanying us through the process. And in the end, the burden for healing is on Him, not us.

Step three: the prayer selection

This step answers the question, 'What kind prayer is needed to help this person?" What lies behind this question is an even more fundamental question: what does God want to do at this particular time for this person?

A secret to healing prayer is that it comes from God having already touched our spirits; it is agreement with God about His will. This is in part what it means to receive an anointing for healing prayer in a specific situation. An anointing is a knowing in the deepest part of our hearts that God wants to heal someone.

Page 206

There are many ways in which we may pray for healing. I have already mentioned several different kinds of prayer used in divine healing; prayers of petition and intercession, words of command, and so on. These different types of healing prayers fall into two categories, petitions directed toward God and words that we receive from God and speak to a condition or a demon.

In a prayer directed towards God I always ask God about how I should intercede for a sick person. Remember, the key to answer prayer is praying according to the will of God. If we believe that He hears us and cares about our needs, we may with confidence approached Him and asked how we should pray. Sometimes, even when I have a clear understanding of the cause of a condition, I am not sure about how to pray specifically. In these instances I pray in my mind, "Lord, I know you want to heal this person please show me how to pray for him."

Words of command

Sometimes I sense God telling me to speak a word of command when praying for divine healing. The words, usually a very short sentence, come out before I consciously formed them. Words of command come with a burst of faith. I feel the confidence and power of God rise in my heart and release it to my speech. Typically I will lay hands near the afflicted area and say, "I break the power of this condition in the name of Jesus," or "stop it"! These prayers are very short and very effective.

I often use a word of command because that is more of the model I see used by Jesus and the early church disciples. I previously spoke about the policemen analogy. I believe we are policemen of sorts commanding bad guys to stop. And, we are called to speak to mountains as outlined in Mark 11:20. We are commissioned to exercise power and authority over the works of the devil and the command is one very effective way to do it.

John continues:
I do not understand how the word of command works, but I can describe what my experience has been. In some instances I speak directly to evil spirits, commanding them to leave. In other instances I seem to be speaking to the condition itself. Despite my lack of clarity about what actually takes place through a word of command, it is certainly biblical, for Jesus frequently healed through it.

A third type of authoritative word involves what Scripture calls a prayer of rebuke in which demons are cast out or their power is broken. In a prayer of rebuke we break a demons hold on a person, containing their power, and eliminate their presence. Rebuking an evil spirit is similar to a word of command. In Mark 9:25, it says:
"When Jesus saw that the crowd was running to the scene, He rebuked the evil spirit. You deaf and mute spirit He said, I command you, come out of him and never enter him again."

Here the simple command is directed toward the evil spirit. I usually say, "In the name of Jesus, I rebuke you evil spirit. You have no part in Jane's life."

Page 211
Step four: the prayer engagement

This step answers the question, "how effective are our prayers?" The prayer engagement consists of prayer, laying on of hands, and when needed further interviewing. The way we pray is determined by our diagnostic decision and prayer selection.

When someone suffers from a physical affliction I try to put my hand near the location of their hurt or suffering. In the case of a woman with a more intimate malady like breast cancer, I ask her husband or another woman to place hands near the area in need; then I place my hands on top of theirs. Or, if I am alone with a woman, I will ask her to cross her hands over the affected area and I place my hands on hers. It is important to treat people with respect so they maintain their dignity.

After laying on hands, I pray aloud that the Holy Spirit will come and minister to the person. My prayers are quite simple; "Holy Spirit, I invite you to come on this person and release your healing power or Holy Spirit, come and show us how to pray."

On page 212 John goes into his description of some of the manifestations of the Holy Spirit he has witnessed as he has prayed for people. I have also witnessed all of these:

People respond to the power of the Holy Spirit in ways that are not always predictable. These "manifestations," or phenomena that occur among people in response to God's power and truth, vary in form: falling over, shaking, sobbing, laughing, spontaneous praise and worship.

John goes on to elaborate on some of these manifestations in pages 212 through 223. Where he concludes with:

...we should not be surprised by how the Holy Spirit manifests Himself to people. Unusual emotional and physical phenomena are common in Scripture, church history and today. These experiences do not ensure healing; healing is an internal work of the Holy Spirit. Finally we do not pray over people for these experience; we pray for God's power to come and heal them.

When we recognize God's healing power is on the person for whom we are praying, we are able to bless His presence and pray for more power. This is a fundamental principle for effective healing prayer: honor what the Lord is doing and usually He will do more. Also when we recognize the Holy Spirit is on people, we can help them to understand and cooperate with His work in their lives. Some people do not realize that God may manifest himself in these ways, so they become passive or frightened, unable to receive their healing. When I am unsure about what the Holy Spirit is doing I ask questions. "Do you feel anything now...a warmth or tingling? Is God speaking to you?" Some people have so little faith for healing that even when the Holy Spirit manifests himself powerfully, they do not believe that He is healing. I encourage them not to be afraid to open their hearts to God and receive his healing power. I pray for a while, and talk with them, then pray again.

Page 224

Taking time to ask questions during the prayer engagement step may also indicate the root cause is different from what was initially thought. For example it is not unusual to determine during the diagnostic step that a person needs inner healing....

After a couple of minutes of praying I will check back with the person as to how they're doing. I will ask if they're feeling anything and if their pain level is the same or less. I also ask them to be honest and not try to make me feel good with their response. No matter what their answer, with their permission I continue to pray. If more time is available I sometimes will go on for 20 minutes or more.

What I would like to get most Christians away from is the "close the eyes and ask God to help the person" type of prayer. I would like to see a proactive, authoritative, and interactive prayer time where we are actually looking for something to happen in the here and now.

John goes into more details about manifestations of the Holy Spirit and dealing with the demonic through page 234.

Page 235
Step five

The last step in the healing procedure is post prayer direction. This answers the questions, "What should this person do to remain healed?" And "What should this person do if he or she was not healed?" When people are not healed I reassure them that God loves them and encourage them to seek more prayer. Usually this means directing them to a prayer team or kinship group in which they may receive longer-term prayer.

If the sickness was rooted in a sin or fault that the person has revealed to me, I will encourage them as Jesus said to the woman taken in adultery to "go and sin no more."....and to get help if it is an ongoing problem. If it was brought by an oppressive spirit I will instruct them to "resist the devil and he (the spirit) must flee from you," as stated in the book of James. This is important because a sickness brought by an evil spirit can try to return. The person must take responsibility for their own well being and healing by filling their minds with the truth of God, submitting their lives to Him and resisting the evil one.

I want to encourage you to take small steps and begin the process of making yourself available to be used by God to help hurting people. Don't be discouraged because you don't know

enough, have some fear or if it feels difficult to begin. Just start somewhere, asking God to give you the grace and compassion to continue. If in the next few months you only pray for one person who gets help, celebrate that and continue. If you pray for 10 people who don't seemingly get help, continue also. At the right time God will show up and do some amazing things and you will be glad you went forward.

Even if we don't see anything or the person being prayed for doesn't experience anything doesn't mean nothing is happening. **It is impossible to pray and have absolutely nothing happened, because God is in our prayers.** More than we know is happening in the spiritual realm when we pray for people. As mentioned before I strongly suggest a healing course given by someone who actively prays for people on a regular basis and sees results. But even if you can't find a course, determine to make a start.

Because some may be curious I will share about how I pray.

The following is a shortened and very general outline of how I pray for people. It is my rough outline and my basic model. Don't take this as the "method" or the "technique." I do the following things because they are scriptural and work for me and have worked for many people that I have prayed for. They fit me, my personality and the current season of God's grace in my life. But, the bottom line is slowly learning to be **led by the Spirit** and trying to do what the Lord is doing and in the way He would like us to do it.

In the final analysis, all prayer is good. Whatever causes a person to feel loved and encouraged by us and by God usually is a good thing.

I try to make the process of praying as simple as possible and I have tried to make it simple for you also.

Before praying I usually remind myself that God is good and delights in helping people. I go into a prayer time expecting something good to happen every time.

When approached by a person coming for prayer in a church setting, I usually introduce myself and try to remember their name (I wish I did this better). I smile and try to put them at ease.

In my heart I am already asking the Holy Spirit for guidance and information as to how He would like to help this person. I usually ask them something like "what would you like Jesus to do for you today." This puts the focus on Jesus and not on me. Sometimes I will say "if Jesus was standing in front of you what would you ask Him to do?" This sometimes helps a person come to a place of saying "I would ask Jesus to heal me now," and might move them towards faith for that happening.

After I have found out what the problem is and what they would want Jesus to do for them, I try to pause with them to listen to the Holy

Spirit for a few seconds in order to decide how and what to pray. I will stretch this pause out a little longer if I'm feeling unsure and I may ask more questions. If I don't hear or sense anything specific at all from the Holy Spirit, I go with my gut feelings on how to pray. (Please see "A healing prayer tool box" in Chapter 15 for much more on this.)

I begin to draw from what the Holy Spirit is showing me and the information I have available up to that point.

To me, injuries are usually the easiest to pray for because they usually do not have a spiritual (demonic) root to them that needs to be investigated. So, if a person injured his back by lifting something the wrong way my prayer would be fairly short and simple. I would ask permission to place my hand on the affected area or if it is a person of the opposite sex I would place my hand on a shoulder. I would then speak to the area of injury and say something like "back be healed in the name of Jesus, pain leave now, muscles, discs, vertebrae be restored."

Before praying for any long term sickness or disease I usually ask when it began in order to see if there was something that happened at the time it started. Sometimes I will ask the person to close their eyes and asked the Lord to show them anything that might have taken place at the time the sickness started. If they don't understand what I mean I will explain to them that some problems are rooted in trauma, accidents, crisis or conflicts with people. I usually don't get specific words of knowledge about these things so I allow the Lord to show the person individually.

Often forgiveness will need to take place before healing can happen. I usually ask the person to close their eyes and asked the Lord if He would show them anyone they need to forgive. Then if they don't know how to do it I lead them in a prayer of forgiveness.

It is commonly believed that some sicknesses and emotional problems are caused by spirits so I will often command the spirit causing the sickness to stop or leave the person such as a spirit of cancer, depression, fear, anxiety etc. I very often revert to prayers of authority. I make them short and simple but authoritative because that's the way Jesus and the early disciples did it. For instance for a disease like cancer, I will say with authority "spirit of death and cancer, we break your power and rebuke you and command you to leave _____ in the name of Jesus!" "Cancer go, leave ___'s body now in and through the mighty name of Jesus Christ!"

Often I will ask the person to personally come against the spirit of sickness or infirmity themselves by saying something like "spirit of sickness, fear, etc. I command you to leave me in the name of Jesus." I do this because people need to take ownership over their own body and anything afflicting them. Then I will pray for and release the healing power of God to them. I usually picture this as the power of the Holy Spirit coming out of me and into the person.

Often during a prayer session I will ask the person how they are doing. As the person reports back to me what is or is not going on I determine what to do next. As mentioned before I celebrate any improvement. I no longer pray once and that's all. I feel I owe the person in front of me more time and more than one prayer. Sometimes I will pray three or more times in the same prayer session, just like Bill and James mentioned in previous chapters.

After this I will usually talk with the person regarding what just happened and anything I sense the Lord leading me to say in conclusion or what I sense God might be saying to the person for their well being.

I always, always try to leave the person encouraged that God loves them and will never give up on them or their problem. If necessary I will invite them back for prayer as often as they feel they need it. And, very importantly, I advise them to seek God themselves and prayer from other people. I try not to have people become dependent on me.

As mentioned before you can glean from other people's experience in this type of prayer by reading the books in the bibliography.

14

Preparing & staying prepared to pray for others

As we progress in being equipped to pray for others our thinking and lifestyle may need adjusting. We must keep in the forefront of our mind that we are as qualified as any other Christian to pursue healing for others. Although the equipping process is ongoing and will continue till the end of our earthly life, we can try to live ready to help and pray. We should try to remember that we, the church and body of the Lord Jesus Christ, are His main plan to spread the Gospel of the Kingdom (which includes healing and freedom) to every person. Therefore we should continue to be trained and equipped and hang out with others of like mind.

By the grace of God, we, the church, the body of Christ, should eventually be able to say to the world what Jesus said... "If you don't believe me for the words that I say, **believe me on account of the works**."

Getting closer to the point of being able to say this is becoming more and more important today as we encounter those of other religions, atheists, agnostics and people in the occult. Words just will not do it for them and rightly so. Jesus still wants to give them more than words! Even after being healed or experiencing a miracle an unbeliever still may refuse to believe in Christ but they will have more to give account of to God about their unbelief.

At this very moment there are thousands of people just like you in churches in the USA and around the world who are demonstrating His words and His works with power and effectiveness. I know of several places, one in particular, Bethel Church in Redding Ca., in which healings and the miraculous are part of their normal Christian culture and lifestyle! (www.ibethel.org) I strongly encourage you to look in on this website or their media site www.ibethel.tv

So, how to progress further toward the goal of being used by the Lord in this type of ministry? Here are some tips I hope will be helpful:

1.**Stay close to the Lord,** spending time with Him and getting to know His love for you, His heart and His voice. Tune in to what moves His heart for the lost, broken, hurting and sick. Dialog with Him during times of simply soaking in His presence, worship and journaling. Intimacy with the Lord results in us being filled so that we can spill over to others. Listen, He has some really good things to say to us, words of encouragement, love and destiny! Jesus' habit was to go from times of intimacy with His Father in a quiet place into the world and its problems with confidence to confront the works of darkness. Sounds like a pretty good model to me.

2. **Follow your heart because what moves Him has been placed there.** One of the things God places in our hearts is a desire to see Jesus' works in the here and now. This is part of our spiritual DNA, our destiny and calling and its right there in your heart! Also, your Godly dreams for your future are placed in your heart and your friend Jesus wants you to reach them. He likes your goals and dreams and wants to co-labor with you in achieving them. As you look around you in your workplace or the marketplace become more aware of God gently tugging you towards a person in need. A few kind and friendly words of interest and compassion for someone could result in a miracle encounter.

3. **Review and rehearse** over and over again who you are in Him and how great and powerful He is in you, with you and for you! Believe He wants to co-labor with and use you! Remember that you are part of his plan to change the world around you.

4. **Be brave** and take small steps outside your comfort zone. John Wimber said "Faith is spelled R I S K." Most of the times that I have seen God do amazing things, were times when I was at least a little bit afraid. I am learning to do it afraid. Get involved with others who are already taking risks…faith and courage rub off! Any attempt of offering help or love to another person is good even if it is a bit scary.

5. **Read other books** as well as the Bible. As mentioned, two authors who have helped me move forward in my pursuit of healing for others are

John Wimber (try "Power healing" & "Power Evangelism") and anything by Bill Johnson, (especially "When Heaven Invades Earth" & "The Supernatural Power of a Renewed Mind"). Read the life stories of revivalists and other men and women whom God has used in powerful ways. You'll find them to be very ordinary people also who simply hunger after God and made themselves available to be used. **Check out Randy Clark's website**, www.globalawakening.org   Attend one of his healing schools. Or read any of his books.

6. **Get trained** to be part of a prayer/healing ministry at your church or in your area. Find out where there is a local "Healing Room" ministry. This is an amazing worldwide ministry that will train you and put you in the action. Google healing rooms to find one in your area.

7. **Don't concentrate on the negatives** of healing prayer i.e. not all people getting healed, the disappointments, your perceived failures…keep going forward, knowing He is with you and victories are coming. Concentrate on what He is doing, not on what is not happening! Keep celebrating when even the smallest answer to prayer takes place.

8. **Keep asking God for more.** Don't be satisfied with powerlessness in your church or in yourself. Seek God for more of his heart towards the lost and hurting. Seek him for more of his presence, power and gifting. Go after the gifts that are available from him.

9. **Stay hungry, desperate and unsatisfied.** I have probably seen more of the miraculous in the last 10 years than many people. But, because I know there is more; because Jesus healed all who came to Him; I refuse to be satisfied. I have had only one occasion when **all** who asked for prayer reported being healed. I am very grateful to God for that but I refuse to be satisfied until more occasions like that take place. God honors us when we are grateful for what He is doing and hungry for more! And because there is always more with God, stay hungry!

10. **Ask for gifts.** Paul said to earnestly desire the gifts of the Spirit. Find out what they are and ask God to give them you so that you can help others. (1 Cor 12:4; 14:1)

15

A Healing Prayer Tool Box

Although it is only God who heals, He wants to co-labor with us in the healing process. I picture this as a master carpenter teaching his apprentice how to do amazing carpentry. God teaching us which tools to use and how to use them most effectively is one of the goals of co-laboring with Christ. As apprentices we must learn about the tools and continue to be "tuned in" to the master as to which ones to use and when and how to use them.

Jesus said often "....I only do what I see the Father doing...." I believe this is both specific and general. Generally, His father was always caring for people, healing the sick, injured, broken hearted, demonized....setting the captives free etc. But, He did more specific things like making mud and placing it in the eyes of the blind man....some of those more specific and general things follow along with other tools from scripture.

We must believe that God **wants** to heal...that it is His **nature and character** to do so, and that He wants to use us. We are empowered by the Holy Spirit and commissioned to heal today. If we wait until we are perfect, faultless, fearless or more holy we will be waiting the rest of our lives.

After tuning in to what God is doing or wants to do we then have options as we are led by him:

1. **The principle of laying hands on the sick.** This is the most common method used in the Scriptures but it is not exclusively used. Prayers from any distance are equally as effective if offered in faith.

2. **Anointing with oil and the prayer of faith.** In the book of James we see he was addressing believers who were to use this type of prayer for other believers. We anoint and **pray believing** ("the prayer of faith") that the Lord will answer. Remember what I said about believing while praying and after praying. Faith can be a choice and a decision we make. You can choose to believe.

3. **The exercise of power and authority...Jesus gave it...we have it...we can use it.** This usually takes the form of a command in the name of Jesus. i.e. "pain leave, back be straightened, cancer go, ears be healed and opened etc. Often this can include rebuking or "binding" an evil or unclean spirit which we sense has brought the problem through oppression and commanding it to leave the person.

4. **The giving and receiving of forgiveness.** Some illnesses are rooted in past trauma and hurts resulting in bitterness, anger or resentment against those who have hurt them. Helping them through the steps of forgiveness is important. Unforgiveness is the root cause or entryway of many sicknesses and diseases.

5. **Prayers of intercession**...i.e. "God, we ask that you will come by your Holy Spirit and rest on ____. Touch and heal them...." etc. Begin looking for evidences of His presence. Some people will feel heat or a wave of warmth coming over them. Some will experience electricity/tingling like feelings. Some may start to shake. Some may be overwhelmed by the presence of God and cannot stand up any longer. The presence of the Holy Spirit may be as simple as the fluttering of their eyes or perspiration. Often when I pray a person's countenance will change from heaviness to lightness and a smile will come upon their face. All these may be evidence of the Holy Spirit at work in the person. Honor His presence and ask for more. Almost without exception people experience peace when I pray for them. The same will happen for you

6. **Encouraging them to believe** without bringing guilt for any lack of faith. Mark 11:24 clearly indicates that there should be at least as much believing as there is praying. People need to know that sometimes it will take several prayers with and through several people in order to see the needed result. Healing belongs to the children of God; it is "the children's

bread." We must encourage people not to give up! Contending for something may be difficult but what are the options?

7. **Releasing what is in you.** If we believe we have the Greater One, the same Spirit that raised Christ from the dead living in us, we are actually able to release Him to others through our hands and our prayers and declarations. We may be led to pray as Peter did… "What I have I give to you, in the name of Jesus Christ of Nazareth rise up and walk" or "be healed and free from this affliction" etc. The "Shalom" of God (His peace) can be released for any need.

8. **Believe for them…** Their faith is not always necessary for them to be healed (Lazarus had no faith, being dead. The Centurion's servant may have had no faith but his master did etc). I make it a policy to walk away from a time of healing prayer believing for the person and thanking God for it, whether I see or feel anything or not.

9. **Praying for others while standing on the truth of God's word** while reminding ourselves of who He is, who you are in Christ and that He speaks to and through His children, that He leads us in our prayers, that His word is alive and active and that his promises are true regardless of the circumstances, is important. As the Holy Spirit leads, pray scriptures and promises of God for others. We are told to take and use the sword of the Spirit, the Word of God as a powerful weapon. Making His words our words, we can use them with the power and authority He has given us! Sometimes just speaking the promises of God over a person can bring amazing results.

10. **Bring the person into an active role in their own healing** by encouraging them to "Submit to God, resist satan (evil spirits, sickness) and He must flee…" James 4:7. This is especially important when people experience healing and then the sickness or pain returns. I told you about my friend James who was healed but had to do this and to say "no!" to the spirits of affliction, infirmity and pain if the symptoms returned. He had to do this a couple of times and all the symptoms left for good.

16

Our part in The Gospel of the Kingdom

Jesus demonstrated the Gospel of the Kingdom as the rule, reign and dominion of God on earth, in the here and now.

"..As you go preach this message 'the Kingdom of God is at hand…" Matt 10:7

"I will give you the keys to the Kingdom of Heaven…."Matt 16:19

"He sent them to preach the Kingdom of God and heal the sick…" Luke 9:2

"….for your Father has been pleased to give you the Kingdom…." Luke 12:32

"If I drive out demons by the finger of God then the Kingdom of God has come upon you…!" Luke 11:20

"I confer on you a Kingdom as my Father conferred one on Me." Luke 22:29

"For the Kingdom of God is not a matter of talk but of power…." 1Cor 4:20

It is important to view our role in the world from the viewpoint of the Kingdom of God and Heaven. As Bill Johnson likes to put it, we must learn to "pray from heaven to earth." So often we are praying to get something from heaven rather than releasing what is there to the need that is here. After all, if we are seated with Christ at the right hand of the father why shouldn't we pray from that position and from the will of God that is already there?

I believe the "Lord's Prayer" was a present tense prayer, a daily, here and now prayer. In it the Lord mentions "daily bread," alluding to the probability that this was a daily prayer. Also, "deliver us from evil," must be a present tense prayer or declaration. The way I pray is, "Your kingdom, **come now**! Your will, **be done now**, just as it is in heaven!" I believe it is a releasing prayer and when we pray it we release the Kingdom and the will of God as it is in heaven now.

The same word "come" was used by the Centurion in Matthew 8:9. He was describing the authority he believed Jesus had to command things to happen. He says, "...I say to this man come and he comes." So I believe The Lord's Prayer to be a declarative prayer; "Your Kingdom COME!" When I go into a prayer session with someone, I go into it with the attitude that I have been given authority to advance the Kingdom of God now. That means I am working together with God to bring the rulership and dominion of God to bear in this situation. You can also.

In Matthew 28:19 Jesus says these parting words to his disciples before He was taken up into heaven:

> All authority has been given to me in heaven and on earth. Go therefore and make disciples of all the nations baptizing them in the name of the father and of the son and of the Holy Spirit, teaching them to **obey all things that I have commanded you**; and I am with you always, even to the end of the age.

We must ask ourselves this question; if all authority has been given to Jesus, how can our enemy have any authority at all. If satan does exercise authority it has to be illegally and probably because people allow him to exercise it.

We give him authority over us the same way as in the garden when Adam and Eve agreed with his lies! When he lies and we agree we are inviting oppression to come in. Remember, when the devil lied and tempted Jesus in the wilderness, He resisted with the truth.

I believe it is up to the church to bring the authority of heaven to bear upon any authority that the enemy tries to usurp. We do this by recognizing his works and destroying them by the power and authority which we have been given by Jesus. Isn't this what Jesus did?

Please note also that in this passage Jesus said to teach all future disciples to **obey everything** that He had **commanded** them. **We must remember that He <u>commanded</u> his disciples to "heal the sick, raise the dead, cast out demons and <u>declare that the Kingdom of God is at hand.</u>**

This is as much of a command to obey as his commands to love our neighbor, give to the poor, pray, worship etc., none of these are optional. But very rarely do we hear about obeying the **command** to heal the sick, raise the dead and drive out demons.

Why? I believe it is because we have not been preaching and teaching the Gospel of the Kingdom as Jesus and his disciples did. I know I've said this before but this is what **we** desperately need to get, so I will re-emphasize it again.

The gospel that Jesus and the early disciples preached was the Gospel of the Kingdom and included healing and deliverance. The Gospel that I was taught to preach was the Gospel of forgiveness of sins and eternal life through Jesus Christ. And although this is the most important part of the Gospel of the Kingdom there is more that we need to be teaching, preaching and demonstrating.

The Kingdom that Jesus brought was meant to grow and have dominion in the whole earth. We, the church, his body, are His main way of doing this. Here are some things to learn and remind ourselves about as we move forward in bringing the Kingdom and will of God to Earth.

His view of us...our view of ourselves

Finding our true identity and worth in Christ and in His Kingdom is essential. We **need to begin to really like who we really are!** Do you see yourself as holy, righteous and sinless in His sight...a child of God, a son or daughter and not a slave...an heir and co-heir of the Kingdom of God with Christ...seated with Jesus' at the right hand of the father...sent into the world with the same power and authority as Jesus.....able to do the works of Jesus?

Review and rehearse your true identity according to heaven's viewpoint. Go through the New Testament and realign your thinking about yourself with God's thinking about you. Begin to see yourself as not only forgiven but dearly loved, totally accepted, part of a wonderful and powerful heavenly family, fully backed by God and heaven, no longer "just a sinner saved by grace," but a saint and a new creature with all the resources of heaven at your disposal.

Stop viewing yourself as not so holy, not completely righteous; a sinful little Christian, an unworthy slave, not inheriting anything, (not in this life at least), not really having much power or authority and of course not able to do any of the works of Jesus. "As a man thinks in his heart so is he." What you think about yourself and what you say about yourself causes you to become that person.

Please indulge me as I use a silly example.

What if you were an aide to the President of the United States? And you came into the Presidents bedroom to find him huddled under the covers, afraid to come down to the oval office.

You say, "Mr. President it's time to enter into the work of the day." But he says , "I'm not sure I can do it, I'm not sure I really am qualified to be the commander in chief and leader of the free world, I don't **feel** like it today. I probably am not qualified because I made a lot of mistakes in the past; some of my policies haven't worked."

You say, "But sir you were elected and it's already in the history books that you are the President and Commander, beside the people have elected you regardless of your past mistakes." But, he says, "I know that mentally but today I don't **feel** like I have any power or authority. A lot of my critics don't think I'm much of anything and I am tending to agree with them." You say, "But sir the entire government, judicial system and congress are ready to back you up." "Where does it say that?" he says. "Why it's in the Constitution, sir." He says, "I know it's written in there but it's just so hard to believe…"

Silly example? Farfetched maybe, but that's how many of us think, speak and act every day.

Jesus says we are sons, but we sometimes think and act as slaves. Jesus calls us friends, but we sometimes think and act like strangers. He says I give you power, we think and act powerless. He has made us kings, and we think and act like paupers.

We were born-again into a royal family and we have a powerful kingdom at our disposal. We have been given power and authority to exercise on behalf of the King! We can exercise that power on behalf of the reigning King of Kings and Lord of Lords! We simply must get more of an understanding of our place in the Kingdom.

Power and authority.

Because of its importance I will expand upon an example I made earlier in the book.

A modern day example of Kingdom authority that believers possess might be a policeman. He would have little power of himself, if he were not personally selected by the city or state government. When a bad guy sees a policeman, the bad guy usually runs and hides because he knows the policeman has all the power and authority of the government behind him to shoot him if necessary. He can also arrest him, handcuff him and bring him before the magistrates to execute justice.

But a policeman must be fully aware every day of just who he is. He can't waver in his governmentally given authority. Nor can he go out in his own authority and say, "Stop in the name of me!" He can't reason with the thief saying "now you really need to stop what are doing, the police department doesn't look favorably on it." No, every morning he puts on his uniform, his badge and gun. When he steps out his front door **he knows who he is**. Our towns and neighborhoods would be overrun with thieves and murderers if the police were unsure of who they were and were not exercising their authority.

We too must over and over again rehearse just who we are, if we are to take back what the thief (satan) has stolen from us and the hurting people around us. Just as policemen are enforcers of the law, **we must learn to take our place as enforcers of the justice of the Kingdom of God.**

If you overheard my prayers for people you would hear me often say things that closely resemble "Stop in the name of the law!" Only, I would be saying "stop in the name of Jesus!"

His Kingdom mission on the earth....our mission

Jesus came for several reasons. To "...Do the will of my father...to seek and save those who are lost... and to destroy the works of the devil." Remember, Jesus boldly declared his mission in Luke 4:18 "... to preach good news to the poor...to heal the brokenhearted...to Proclaim freedom for prisoners and recovery of sight for the blind, to release the oppressed, and proclaim the year of the Lord's favor."

Jesus fully intended that this Kingdom mission would be carried on in and through us, his followers. Didn't He say "As the father has sent me so I send you"?

His way of being, our way of being

It should be obvious that Jesus transformed people and situations around him by bringing the Kingdom of God to bear. Only out of His life of intimacy with His father was Jesus able to do this. Learning to be with Him in order to know Him and affect others is important. Jesus went from intimacy with his father, face time with his dad, to confront the powers of darkness.

His results...our results...People and situations changed!

Blind, crippled, deaf, lame, demon possessed, brokenhearted, prisoners, captives, lost, depressed, spiritually and naturally dead...changed by Jesus bringing the Kingdom of God to bear in their lives and situations. When we know who we really are and what our mission is in life, when we get our power and guidance from intimacy with the Him, then we can more effectively do "the works of Jesus and greater works..." and we can begin to expect the same results.

My own personal rehearsal of who I am follows. I don't do all of this all the time but I do a lot of it a lot of the time. Why? Because it is absolutely necessary for my faith, confidence, success **and survival!** I must continually remind myself:

Jesus wants to bring the kingdom of God and the will of God as it is in heaven through me into the present situation.

Jesus has made me worthy of doing these works by his substitutionary, perfect and finished work on the cross for me.

He hears and answers my prayers for myself and for others.

I am a son of God; my Father hears me and I can hear him. In fact He so loves me and others He is anticipating answering my prayers, backing up my statements and declarations.

I can have complete confidence when I pray that my father has heard me and is answering and I can walk away believing even if I see no immediate change! My believing can result in seeing.

I have as much power and authority and favor before my Father as the early disciples had.

Not only is He for me and with me, but He is in me!

The mighty Spirit of the living God dwells in me and desires to be released to others. His Spirit is more powerful than any power of the devil or his minions and their works.

I am called to carry on the mission of Jesus. God wants to use me to intervene on the behalf of hurting people.

When I discern his leading, I can act as He would have acted and expect the same results.

Past disappointments will not make me conclude that the next prayer encounter with someone will also result in disappointment.

17

A Commissioning & Sending

Time to act on who you really are and who He is in and with you!

From the "Message Bible"… Ephesians 1:21-23

…. no name and no power is exempt from His rule. And not just for the time being, but forever. He is in charge of all, **has the final word on everything.** At the center of all this, Christ rules the church. **The church (you), is not peripheral to the world; the world is peripheral to the church (you). The church is Christ's body (us), in which (and through which) He speaks and acts, and by which He fills everything with His presence!**

The works of Jesus were to continue through his followers after his resurrection. In fact his works were to go on forever until the day that Jesus would return.

Eugene H. Peterson is the author of the amazing "Message" Bible. Read carefully what He has to say in his introduction to the book of Acts:

Because the story of Jesus is so impressive...God acting in ways that heal and help and save us...there is a danger that we will be impressed, but only be impressed. As the spectacular dimensions of this story slowly (or suddenly) dawns upon us, we could easily become enthusiastic spectators, and then let it go at that, become admirers of Jesus, generous with our oohs and aahs, and in our better moments inspired to imitate Him.

It is Luke's task to prevent that, to prevent us from becoming mere spectators to Jesus, fans of His message:

The story of Jesus doesn't end with Jesus. It continues in the lives of those who believe in him. The supernatural does not stop with Jesus. Luke makes it clear that these Christians he wrote about were no more spectators of Jesus than Jesus was a spectator of God... they are in on the action of God, God acting in them, God living in them, which also means, of course God living in **us**.

God wanted the book of Acts to be open-ended and to continue until Jesus returns. Therefore, I believe that Jesus is saying to you, the church, the first team, the following:

I want you to know who you really are! I want you to know who I really am in and for and with you! As you learn these things and absorb them into your mind, soul and spirit, you will think and act from a place of faith, peace and power!

I, Jesus became a **perfect Savior** for you. I acted in sinless and perfect obedience to our Father in your place; therefore you can stand before Me at peace because you are holy and righteous in My sight. And because of that you can know that you are absolutely and unconditionally loved because you are in Me. You can rest in my love and acceptance of you and in your position of holiness because of My finished, perfect work at the cross. You are qualified to be used by Me because of what I have done, not by how perfect you are.

And because I died and you died with Me, your sins, mistakes, and shortcomings have all been covered by My sacrifice. So, you are forgiven, loved and accepted, past, present and future. In fact you are so accepted that you have access to the very throne room of my Father and **are seated with Me in the place of honor, authority** and power at His right hand. We can co-labor together from this place of authority!

 Live free of guilt, condemnation and accusations which are from the enemy. Take authority over and reject those thoughts and take your place as a holy, righteous, beloved, and empowered son or daughter.

I am not only your Lord, King and Savior but I am also **your friend!** Your father is not only the Sovereign and Almighty but also your **abba-daddy!** My Holy Spirit is not only your comforter and guide into truth but also **your companion empowerer who lives in you!**

Remember this! What the first Adam gave away to the devil (power, dominion and authority) I, the **last Adam**, took back by my perfect obedience and sacrifice as the Lamb of God and I have given it back to you. Therefore because I am **fully** in you and have transferred to you power and authority, forgiveness, love and peace, you can now give all that and all of me away to the hurting world around you.

You, the church, my body, have **plenty** to give; me in you, with all the love, compassion, mercy, healing and freeing power that I possess! **Give me away! Release all that I am!**

Don't be afraid, I am with you! Take action! Go, because I am sending you as I sent my disciples, to bring justice and rescue those in bondage to sin, disease, pain, heartache and the works of the enemy...do as I did, look for the devils works and destroy them through me!

18

Important excerpts from John Wimbers' book "Power Evangelism"

From the introduction to his book:

On October 6, 2006 Christianity Today published the results of a survey titled "The Top 50 Books that have Shaped Evangelicals." The editors and a distinguished panel of 62 authors decided that Power Evangelism was the 12th most influential book just behind Richard J. Foster's Celebration of Discipline and ahead of Josh McDowell's Evidence That Demands a Verdict.

The premise of this book is that Scripture teaches that Power Evangelism - the proclamation and supernatural demonstration of the kingdom of God - is the most effective way of winning followers to Christ.

In a previous chapter I told the "Hiccup Story." This story of my encounter with three young people in a Taco shop illustrates to a small extent what power evangelism can be. In this encounter I co-labored with God to bring about a cure for the girls hiccups, give encouraging words of knowledge (insights) from God to her and to her friends and subsequently lead them all to faith in Jesus Christ.

I believe that it was the combination of healing and words of knowledge which led to their coming to Jesus. I'm not sure if the result would have been the same if I had simply approached them and started to try to persuade them about Jesus. I feel that God showed His love, care and here and now reality to them through the healing and words of knowledge and because of these things they felt quite comfortable in believing.

It is God's desire that all Christians, in their efforts to win the lost, should avail themselves of **every means of God necessary** to do it most effectively. If Jesus and his disciples combined proclamation **and** demonstration of the Gospel of the Kingdom as their main "method" of evangelism why shouldn't we?

If you are still reading this book, it indicates that you have a strong desire to continue in this direction.

Here are some of the passages from John Wimber's book that have strongly affected me.

In describing our use of power and authority John says:

> Power is the ability, the strength and the might to complete a given task. Authority is the right to use the power of God.

> Our difficulty is that we have not learned to receive or give orders. To a great extent, we practice a cosmetic Christianity because we misunderstand our initial call to Christ. We think that the key to maturity and power is to be "good." We then focus on our behavior. But our behavior never meets the high standards of Christ's righteousness.

> I did this for years. By focusing on my behavior, I was in constant turmoil, because my behavior was never good enough and rarely met God's (or my own) standards of righteousness. I first believed in Christ because I was not good enough, yet after becoming a Christian, I still struggled in my own strength with not being good enough. So, I was always struggling with guilt.

> Then one day, I fell to my knees and asked God to help me. I sensed Him respond, "Since you can do nothing without Me, how much help do you want?" Then He said, "The issue is not being good, it is being God's. Just come to Me, and I'll provide goodness for you."

Over the next five years God showed John the following:

God had good works prepared for me, but they were His works and I could not do them for Him. He told me that I needed to begin to listen to His voice rather than try to distill the Christian life down to a set of rules and principles.

John goes on to show that listening and obeying the Lord in what he was told to do was a key to naturally becoming a better person and bringing the power of the kingdom to others. He goes on to say: "As the Centurion did we must learn how to hear and believe Jesus commands if we expect to be the vehicles of signs and miracles for the kingdom."

He continues to describe a phrase that he has coined and is used extensively in many Christian circles; the "power encounter."

An analogy that may help us understand what I mean by the term "power encounter" is found in nature. When warm and cold fronts collide, violence ensues: thunder and lightning, rain or snow -- even tornadoes or hurricanes. There is a conflict and the resulting release of energy.

Power encounters are much like that. When the kingdom of God comes into direct contact with the kingdom of the world (when Jesus meets satan), there is conflict. Usually, what ensues is disorderly, messy and difficult for us to control.

An example of the application of the term "power encounter" can be when a person who is demonically oppressed is confronted by a believer who knows his authority and power. When the believer under the guidance of the Holy Spirit prays against the oppression a direct assault on satans' kingdom takes place. The Kingdom of God prevails and the person is freed from the oppression.

John talks about hindrances which can prevent a believer from being used by God. I will add a few that I have discovered:

Fear. Our enemy does not want us to be used by God. Fear can be a primary weapon. Most fears are not grounded in fact. Fear of rejection is one of them. I have probably talked to hundreds of people in the marketplace about Jesus. Very few have rejected me. And those that have rejected me have pretty much just said "no thanks." Remember, God has promised us the Holy Spirit to tell us what to say at these times.

Fear of failure is another. What if nothing happens? I have had to keep in mind that success or failure is in the hands of the Lord. And I have learned that there can be neither without trying. A good question to ask ourselves is "so what's the worst thing that can happen if I fail?" I assure you we will not die and the world will not come to an end. Most people really appreciate an offer for prayer. And if we leave them feeling loved and cared for we have done our job.

Fear of not knowing what to say. You **do** have enough knowledge about Jesus and praying for the sick. And you will get more and more skilled as you go on depending on the Holy Spirit for the words you will need.

Unworthiness. As I have stated earlier God sees you as worthy already. A review of the scriptures about how God views us is necessary.

Many people believe that speaking to others about Jesus, sharing the gospel with or praying for strangers requires special gifting. Most of the New Testament points to the opposite. Regular, ordinary followers of Jesus, doing the things that He did, were the plan and should be the norm.

John Wimber talks about how signs, wonders, miracles and the proclamation and demonstration of the kingdom of God are the bedrock of church planting.

He gives the example of how the Yoido Full Gospel Church, in Seoul Korea, with a membership of 830,000, was launched by Pastor Paul Yongi Cho. He states:

> The beginning days of the church was known even then for a constant flow of God's miracle power, its phenomenal growth was the continuation of a trend modeled by Christ: "people brought to Jesus many who had demons in them. Jesus drove out the evil spirits with a word and healed all who were sick". (Matthew 8: 26)

In trying to set the course of his ministry in obedience to Jesus, John tried to determine some things from scripture:

> When I turned to the Bible, I tried to answer three questions. First, how did Jesus evangelize? Second, how did Jesus commission the disciples? Third, in the light of their commissioning how did the disciples evangelize?

These questions and the answers to them from the scriptures should also set the course for our evangelization of the lost. Having read the previous chapters you should come to the same conclusions as John Wimber did. Jesus basically did the following as John Wimber says: first, Jesus preached repentance and the good news of the Kingdom Of God. And secondly He demonstrated it by casting out demons, healing the sick, and raising the dead—which proved He was the Anointed One, the Messiah.

John goes on to talk about how Jesus commissioned the disciples.

> For three years Jesus taught the disciples how to minister from hearts of compassion and mercy, hear the father, grow in dependence on the Holy Spirit, be obedient to God's leading and believe that God performs miracles through (ordinary) men and women.
>
> Jesus commissioned the disciples to bring people fully under his reign into the Kingdom of God. **This is a "kingdom conversion" in which people come into a new reality -- a reality in which the "supernatural" is quite natural**. Thought of this way, conversion involves both a change in the person being born again and a change of citizenship, (leaving the kingdom of satan and entering the Kingdom of God; see 2 Corinthians 5:16 - 17).
>
> The goal of making obedient disciples who are integrated into the body of Christ is a high (if not impossible) ideal apart from God. This is why Christ promised help to fulfill the task: "You will receive power when the Holy Spirit comes on you; and you will be my witnesses in Jerusalem, and in all Judea and Samaria and even to the ends of the earth" (acts 1:8).

What Jesus was saying in effect and what John strongly defends is that the power of the Holy Spirit is essential to carrying out the commission.

John also coined the phrase "divine appointment." This is simply a meeting of a believer with another person for a God ordained purpose. This is what happened to me in the taco shop, on the DMV waiting line and in most of the healings and miracles I have described in this book. It can involve a chance meeting with someone to share a little or a lot about Jesus, a prayer for deliverance, healing, or help of any kind. It involves us taking the risk of stepping into this appointment and seeing where God leads us.

In chapter 17 John tells the story of how a whole household came to the Lord through signs and wonders. It is the story of a Doctor Almedo in Ecuador. He was a professor of philosophy at a university, had written five textbooks in his field and was well known as the author of a booklet on **how to raise the ideal atheist family**.

When an evangelist came to his city his wife and daughter went to one of his meetings and both of them were physically healed and as a result came to Christ. The daughter confronted the father with these words "Daddy, I'm going to prove to you once and for all that there is a God and that Jesus Christ is alive today. I'm going to sing for you in a language I've never learned. Gabriella then proceeded to sing as the Holy Spirit gave her words. She sang in Russian, then German, then Italian, then French, and finally in English." Although this left him shaken he did not convert. It was only when the Lord gave the daughter knowledge about specific sins in his life that the professor dropped to his knees praying "Lord I am a fool," and offered his life to God.

I have mentioned before that healings, miracles, signs and wonders are very much needed today to see the conversion of people of other religions, atheists, satanists and all who have *good reason* not to believe.

In the later chapters of the book John talks about Western mindsets, rationalism and materialistic world views. To put it simply these are the things that affect our concept of Christian living and especially the place for signs wonders and the supernatural. He contrasts Jesus worldview with those of the modern church. He says:

Most Western Christians must undergo a shift in perception to become involved in a signs and wonders ministry -- a shift towards a worldview that makes room for God's miraculous intervention... it is difficult for us to recognize something we have not seen before. When we first see it, we do not comprehend it. Seeing in this respect is a learning process that takes place over a period of time...I had to go through a process of learning to see the Kingdom of God, of adjusting my worldview, as I began a signs and wonders ministry.

We have to be careful not to scoff or rationalize away a report of the miraculous happening today. There is a strong tendency among Western Christians to have a "seeing is believing" mentality. Throughout Scripture believing resulted in seeing and not vice versa.

I love to give testimonies and reports of the miraculous healings I see. I also enjoy watching the different reactions on people's faces. Even some people who know me and believe that I'm a credible person, simply have a lot of doubt about what I share. I know several who take an "I would have to be there" attitude when they hear me talk about the miraculous. I understand where they're coming from but I pray that their eyes would be open to believe and see into the Kingdom. Some actually get offended when I share the truth about Jesus healing all who came to him....whats up with that?

John continues and explains that the parameters of our thinking need to shift along with our expectations and He cautions about hardening our hearts:

A hard heart that is closed to the supernatural cannot see or hear the secrets of the Kingdom...The key to seeing the Kingdom of God and doing the works of Christ, is in opening our hearts more fully to his Spirit.

But the one who received the seed that fell on good soil (an open heart) is the man who hears the word and understands it. He produces a crop, yielding 100, 60 or 30 times what was sown. (Matthew 13:23).

We see according to our expectations. Many times, our expectations come from conditioning: we are taught to expect certain things in the Christian life and miss what God is doing if He acts outside of our expectations.

An example of this is that we expect people to come to Christ in a certain way. Someone tells them about Jesus and they make a decision. They pray a prayer and receive Jesus. That's the way I came to Christ, but John tells a story that may challenge this preconceived idea:

One evening a woman came home from a party and on entering her house sensed the presence of someone. It frightened her, but she could not find anyone there. Later in her bedroom, she heard a voice. All it said was, "Rosalee." Her friends knew her only as Lee, even though her full name was Rosalee... she turned and saw no one. Then she heard the voice again, "Rosalee." This time she asked "who is it?" "Lord?" "Yes Rosalee. It is time for you to know me." She fell on her knees and received Christ.

In order for us to enter the realm of the kingdom and the supernatural, we must shift our assumptions and align them with the assumptions of Jesus:

Jesus assumed the existence of a God of absolute authority.
Jesus assumed the existence of good and evil spirits.
Jesus believed in both the kingdom of God and the kingdom of Satan.
Jesus assumed that whenever there would be a power confrontation between the two kingdoms, the Kingdom of God would win.
Jesus assumed that whoever came to him for healing or deliverance should get what they came for.
Jesus assumed a kingdom mentality and an attitude of "as it is in heaven" as supremely valuable.

John goes on to say that that we, like Jesus, should be on the lookout for people who are in need around us, both in and out of church:

Jesus saw the people He preached to and healed as "harassed and helpless" victims of injustice who were powerless to help themselves. He linked his healing ministry with ministry to the poor, because He saw both as bringing justice (Matthew 9:35; 11:5; 12:15 -- 21).

I think this is huge! Jesus saw healing and deliverance as social justice right along with feeding the poor, clothing the naked, and visiting those in prison! For too long some of us have exalted **just some** of the things that serve as social justice. But Jesus saw healing as justice, deliverance as justice, raising those who died prematurely as justice.

When I go to the homeless outreach I do my best to bring them the justice that Jesus died for and would want them to have.

One of the most compelling and empowering parts of John Wimber's book is in appendix A. Signs and Wonders in Church History. For anyone who may believe that healings, deliverance, resurrections from the dead, and the miraculous in general ended with the apostles, this is must read stuff! He documents these things from the time of Justin Martyr in the second century through the medieval era, the Reformation and into the modern era.

He quotes Augustine in the fourth century saying "it is sometimes objected that the miracles, which Christians claim to have occurred, no longer happen. The truth is that even today miracles are being wrought in the name of Christ..." Augustine then documents the following healings or miracles; blindness, cancer, paralysis, hernia, injuries, resurrections, and people being delivered from evil spirits.

John gives a wonderful quote from Martin Luther in the 15th century when Luther was asked what to do after physicians had given up on a case of extraordinary "melancholy."

"This must, rather, be an affliction that comes from the devil, and this must be counteracted by the power of Christ with the prayer of faith. It is what we did for a cabinet maker who was similarly afflicted with madness and we cured him."

Spiritual warfare, power and authority, binding and loosing, demonic oppression.

This is an important subject that we've made mention of in previous chapters but have not expanded on adequately. Jesus gives a good overview of spiritual warfare in Matthew 12:22-29, Mark 9:14, Luke 10:13 and in Luke 11:14 -26. A study of these and other scriptures on the demonic is essential to grasp the importance of Jesus' view of the demonic realm.

Rather than attempting to give you a comprehensive presentation of this subject I will recommend two books that I believe can be very helpful.

In Neil Anderson's book "The Bondage Breaker," a very comprehensive overview of lies, spiritual warfare and the believers' authority is given. In referring to the above mentioned scriptures he says "Another target for authoritative prayer is the "strong man" mentioned in Matthew 12:29, Jesus said, referring to Satan and his demons: *"How can anyone enter the strongman's house and carry off his property, unless he first binds the strong man?"*

I also recommend Dr. Ken Blues' book, "Authority to Heal." In it he says; "for Jesus, sickness was not explained in terms of germs or biological malfunctions but in terms of personalized evil. Jesus saw satan as the cause of all kinds of physical suffering. *"On the Sabbath Jesus was teaching in one of the Synagogues and a woman was there who had been crippled by a spirit for eighteen years. She was bent over and could not straighten up at all."* (Luke 13:10:11) Jesus rebuked demons in Mark 9:25 and also rebuked Peters mother-in-law's fever in Luke 4:39. Modern medicine would likely have attributed the fever to an infection; Jesus apparently regarded the fever and the power behind it, as personalized evil. Other diseases in the gospel story which today might be analyzed as deafness, epilepsy or arthritis are linked by Jesus to Satan. Where we see germs behind sickness, Jesus saw Satan's whip." (chapters 3-8)

There have been several people mentioned in this book who, had to take authority over spirits which were causing their sickness. We all must learn more in this important area of ministry.

The believer has been given power over all the works of the enemy. But in order to exercise this power we must be taught and mentored and schooled in these areas. These two books are an essential starting place.

Quotes and Musings

There are several more very important things that I want to share with you but they just don't fit into any of the previously written chapters. So, here they are.

Quotes

Renowned author and teacher Frances MacNutt has written three important books on the topic of healing. His latest, The Healing Reawakening, powerfully documents the birth of healing and miracles in the 1st century. Their near death over the centuries and the reawakening that has taken place over the past few decades is shown. He says:

> The overriding feature of the early church was that simple, uneducated poor people underwent an intense experience of the risen Christ and of the power of the Spirit. This inspired them to go out preaching that the kingdom of God was at hand. They proceeded to make it happen by healing the sick and casting out evil spirits.

On Suffering

> Jesus' passion was to heal: He treated sickness as a curse. Jesus suffered to an extraordinary degree and He promised his followers that they would suffer too. But the suffering we can expect is what will be inflicted upon us by a hostile and fallen world, not the kind

of suffering that happens because we fall apart from within ourselves through spiritual, emotional and bodily sickness. Nowhere do we have a record of Jesus telling sick people who came to him for healing that He was not going to heal them because they're sickness was a blessing sent by his father as a test of patience.

The decline of healing in the church...the near perfect crime

To destroy a belief as central to Christianity as healing, the change had to take place so gradually that Christians didn't even realize that they had lost anything."

We can compare the near death of Christian healing to Napoleon's sad decline." (He was poisoned slowly over many days).

Century by century its life was weakened; by 1900 only certain parts of the church's healing ministry were still alive and moving. Granted, something so central to Christianity could never completely die; we can rejoice that Christians today in different parts of the world are awakening to the glorious vision that Jesus had for his church. But amazingly, most of the body lies still and unresponsive to the powerful encounters of the Holy Spirit that are sweeping into these nontraditional meetings of believers.

When you think about it, this near destruction of divine healing is an extraordinary mystery, because miraculous healing with its twin, the casting out of evil spirits, lay at the very heart of Jesus Christ's mission. For the first of 400 years of church history Christians expected healing to take place when they prayed! How is it possible that something so central to the gospel almost died out?

Ordinary believers heal the sick

We may be tempted to avoid the challenge (to heal the sick) by saying, "Well, the disciples were a unique group specially chosen by Jesus to walk with him." And yet Luke emphasizes that in the eyes of the religious leaders of that day Peter and John were very ordinary. They were simple lay-men, not priests in charge of official prayer; more than that, they were uneducated and therefore humanly unqualified. And besides, the book of Acts goes on to show that it was not just Peter and the other apostles who healed the sick; it was also Christians like Philip, who started out simply as one of seven men chosen to distribute food.

And then came Paul, who also healed the sick and cast out demons. He represented the next generation, someone who had not walked with Jesus in his lifetime. In fact, Luke makes a special point of showing that Paul, who reached out to the gentiles, performed the same kind of miracles as Peter, the leader of the Hebrew believers.

The power of the Holy Spirit

I agree with Francis MacNutt. People have available to them an encounter with the Holy Spirit that will lead to them being witnesses for Jesus **with power**. John the Baptist declared that Jesus would baptize (flood or immerse) us with the Holy Spirit. Jesus promised a baptism (flooding or immersion) of the Holy Spirit. Before He ascended into heaven, Jesus told his followers to wait for the "promise of the father" and on the day of Pentecost the empowering of the church by the Holy Spirit occurred.

Why not get all that is available to us so that we can be as powerful as Jesus wanted us to be? He continues:

> Christians in the early church believed that when they prayed, the Spirit would show up accompanied by powerful manifestations. When Paul traveled to Ephesus, for example, he found a group of disciples who, to his surprise, had not even heard that there is a Holy Spirit (Acts 19:2). "When Paul placed his hands on them, the Holy Spirit came upon them, and they spoke in tongues and prophesied."

> Visible and audible signs of the Spirit's presence such as these were obviously important and this expectancy lasted for another 300 years.

> Over and over, I have seen people experience the graces of (… an immersion by the Holy Spirit ….) in life transforming ways. Many of them were already earnest Christians, but there was more to life in store for them. For some, longstanding moral problems were suddenly overcome through the Spirits help; others began to see the sick healed when they pray; pastors found themselves speaking more personally about Jesus and less about abstract topics. Almost all experienced a much closer personal relationship with Jesus.

Followers of Jesus should earnestly seek the Lord for this!

Best selling author John Eldridge says that most Christians view the Bible as a book of exceptions, saying things like "That was then, that was those people, that is not now." He asks why God would give us a book of exceptions, when it is really a book of examples of what can and should be now.

Best-selling author George MacDonald says that God wants his children to be and do just as Jesus.

Musings and reflections

We must discover that we are the habitation of God himself. We must discover and realize that the same Spirit who raised Jesus Christ from the dead lives in us. He lives in us for our benefit but He desires to be released to others for their benefit. He wants in and He wants out!

The healing of a person's body is a wonderful miracle but it is not the entire miracle. What happens to the person's spirit, soul and emotional well being because of the healing miracle is often miraculous as well. I have seen people become energized, very encouraged and have a deep awareness of God's love for them as a result of being healed.

What we think, believe and speak has probably the most important effect on the quality of our lives than any other thing we can do! Life and death results from these actions. Look at the result of Adam and Eve when they started to think and believe and ultimately act upon the lie that the devil told them. What did Jesus choose to think about, believe and speak to the devil when He was tempted in the wilderness?

The progression of a thought whether it is the truth or a lie will result in an agreement with God or with the devil. This will result in feelings, words and actions of good or bad, positive or negative, victory or defeat. Agreeing with lies is partnering with the demonic because the devil is a liar!

We spend far too much time changing our emotions when we should concentrate on changing the thoughts that lead to our emotions.

When Jesus sent the twelve and the 70 out to heal the sick He didn't say "except for"... there were no exceptions in his statement. There were none that were too sinful, none that were hopeless cases, none that were impossible to heal and none that were excluded. We need to be careful of excluding people because we know some things about their character, personality or behavior.

God is better, more caring, more gracious and compassionate, and more willing to touch and heal people than we think. So we need to begin to change the way we think.

Bill Johnson says, "In many churches today we have restaurant critics who have never cooked a meal." These are people who have not healed the sick, spoken in tongues, used the gifts of the Spirit or driven out the tiniest demon; yet they condemn and criticize any follower of Jesus on the planet who claims they have done these things. It's easy to judge what is not of God yet not have one miraculous thing happen. Now this is hypocrisy."

"I'm never going to eat again because mom burned the biscuits." Silly, but some of us take this attitude when we have a disappointment in the area of praying for someone to be healed. When they're not healed or even get worse and die we can make a vow in our heart saying to ourselves "God doesn't heal today and I'm not going to pray or believe for the sick anymore." We must use past disappointments as a catalyst to press us even further into God and the area of healing. If we give up after the devil has seemingly won, we can be defeated in this area forever.

I wonder what our attitude would have been on the day of Pentecost. Would we have joined with many who said that what was going on couldn't be of God, that it was too bizarre ("they must be drunk")? I wonder how much of God we really miss when we are more worried about excess than going with the flow of what God is doing.

When difficult times come, many people often associate themselves with Job. We must remember that Job lived in a day when the devil was "the god of this world." Jesus said that all power has been given to Him and then He said to us "I give you power over all the power of the devil." We live in the covenant age where the devil has been defeated by Jesus and must yield to us in his name.

In Hebrews 1:30 it says that Jesus is the **exact** representation of God's nature. I think exact means exact, no? When it comes to healing and most everything else, if Jesus did it or said it, why look anywhere else for the will of God?

The devil wants to keep us in bondage to the past with all its guilt, shame and remorse, or in bondage to the future with fear and anxiety. Jesus wants us to stay in the present where everything is pretty good.

Tongues is called the language of the Spirit. Paul thanked God that he prayed in tongues more than everyone else. It is secret and it is direct. Why not use Paul as a good example and seek God for this gift? He also said that we should earnestly desire for greater gifts of the Spirit.

We've really sold ourselves short and limited our abilities when we don't avail ourselves of the things that God wants us to have. Tongues and the gifts of the Spirit are for our benefit and the benefit of others!

One of Paul's primary concerns was that the cross not be emptied of its power. When we begin to reason about things instead of going with what God has already said we begin to make God like us. We err when we try to be logical and reasonable about God's will and desire to release his power to heal and do the miraculous. *We wind up with a very logical and reasonable reason not to see much happen.*

God will offend our mind in order to reveal what is in our hearts. That is why some in the western church have a high level of knowledge and theology but little experience of power. We can become offended by some things that we conclude cannot be of God, thereby revealing an unbelieving heart and missing the very thing God is doing.

An atmosphere of faith in what Jesus wants and wills to do today will produce an atmosphere of miracles and power. The opposite also is true. The Son of God was unable to do very many works except heal a few people in Nazareth because of their unbelief. If we don't create an atmosphere of faith and belief in our churches how can we expect the hurting people to get the help they need? How do we do that? By teaching and declaring that Jesus is the same yesterday today and forever and wills to heal, and by people giving their testimonies of His miracles. Otherwise we risk becoming a Nazareth environment.

The entrance of sickness can be the same as the entrance of sin into the world. Adam and Eve believed a lie, accepted it and made an agreement with the devil. The result was the disastrous fall of man! The devil can still gain access to our lives through lying, if we allow it. Jesus said that He has given us power over all the power of the devil yet, if we accept what the devil is offering we make an agreement with the demonic.

Jesus proved the fact that sickness was from the devil by overturning it every chance He got. Why do we so easily accept sickness as just something that is part of life when Jesus viewed it as part of the devils agenda and something to be destroyed? There was no sickness in the Garden of Eden. It was not meant to be there. It was not God's will for it to be there. It is not God's will for it to be here now. Jesus showed us how to get rid of it; I think we should follow his example.

The church must move from defensive Christianity to a Christianity that is on the offensive. At the first sign of the devils works we can use three R's:

Resist the thing that the devil is trying to give us, basically saying no thank you; Rebuking the demonic messenger saying "Stop It.... now!!"
Renounce the lie that he wants us to buy into and any agreement we have made with that lie.

Release through our prayers and words the healing power of Jesus in us into this situation.

To me, this is the essence of binding and loosing. Saying no to evil and yes to the desires of our loving father.

We have powerful weapons to overcome the forces of evil, however we need to get them out of the closet, clean them up and begin to use them today!

Because I feel that the following is something God wants to bring the church into I will repeat and expand on something I've previously wrote about getting and maintaining healing.

How I try to maintain healing and health.... The following are some things that I do and recommend to you in order to get healed and stay healed. I have been very successful but not perfect in this. My process is in accordance with Scripture, a few of which are: Matthew 8:17, Mark 11:20-24, John 10:10, 1 Peter 2:24, and Acts 10:38.

I have determined to believe that it is the will of God for me to have good health and to be healed when sickness comes. The basis of this is my model of Jesus who healed all who came to him by which I conclude that sickness was not the will of God then and is not the will of God for me now.

Jesus said He has given us (his disciples) power over all the power of the enemy and nothing should harm us. When something begins to harm me I begin to take a prayerful look at it and determine whether it would be something my loving heavenly father would give me or not.... want me to have or not. If it looks more like something the enemy might want me to have I decide to resist. If it falls in the category of something that Jesus would heal I must conclude that it is not the will of God for me to have it.

I then decide not to sign for a package that Jesus is not sending me. I return it to the sender.

I try to remember other testimonies of people who have been healed of these same things. But most of all I remember that Jesus healed all people who came to him of all sickness. I also remember the cross where there is strong evidence that Jesus paid not only for sins but for sickness.

I speak to the sickness and the symptoms to leave me in the name of Jesus Christ of Nazareth. I also receive by faith the healing that Jesus paid for at the cross. If possible I will get another follower of Jesus to pray and agree with me accordingly.

This principle has won out in my life. After many years of chronic headaches I begin taking allergy medications that have alleviated them. Now this was good but I still wanted to be free of taking allergy medications AND headaches. So I made the choice to pray and believe (Mark 11:24) that I was healed and began to wean myself off of the medications. I am happy to report that I have not had any medications or headaches in over a month!

When slight symptoms of headaches tried to come back I said no and declared that I was healed and that they had to go. They did and I am free!

Before I close out this book I must tell this last story: I met Jim in front of the stage as we were wading into the mob of people wanting prayer on Friday night at Journey CC. He was lifting his arms over his head when I asked him if he needed prayer. He said he didn't need prayer because he just got healed. Chronic joint pain in his neck shoulders and arms had just disappeared after my friend Steven prayed for him. I asked if he needed anything else and he said no. So I continued praying for others.

Later, after the service was over I approached him with my friends Karl and James. Again he told the story of how he was completely relieved of joint pain. While he was talking I noticed one hearing aid and then another. He said he was almost totally deaf in one ear and very deaf in the other. So, I offered to pray for his ears which he politely declined indicating that he didn't think it was very important for the Lord to be bothered with.

I assured him that God did not run out of compassion or power and He was still concerned about his hearing. He said okay and I asked him to remove the hearing aids. He did so and one of those "Kazowie" moments that our pastor and teacher Ed has spoken about happened.

After a very brief prayer he got this "deer in the headlights" look and a big smile came to his face! He said something like "WOW I can hear great now, and actually hear better now out of the ear that was the worst!" Question..... why shouldn't all the Jim's we encounter get their hearing healed?....I believe that's what God wants!

On his way out he and Ed met and he pulled the 2 hearing aids out of his pocket and showed them to him.

This is the Jesus I want to present to the entire world.... how about you?

Conclusion

In the preface of this book I said:

> "There is always more to God than we have experienced. To many folks this is a no-brainer statement...." Yeah, of course there's always more to God, duh!" But some folks, me in particular, can sometimes settle into a place of believing that we have pretty much figured God out in most of the important areas. We can get our theology, doctrines and traditional teachings together in a neat package and settle into a place of "knowing God."
>
> And yet, very often God wants to show us there is so much more to Him than we have concluded or figured out. When we hear of things about God and what He might be doing in other places or with other people, we can too easily discount the reports because they don't fit in with our neat package. The result is that we may be limiting God and what He really desires to do and therefore miss out on some extraordinary aspects of His nature.

I've had to ask myself a hard question many times since I became a believer in 1978. The question is "Have I placed God into my neat theological package and limited Him from what He might really want to do in my life and in the lives of others?"

After having read this book you may want to ask yourself the same question. If the things in this book are even a little beyond your realm of belief and application, I urge you take them to God in prayer and ask for His opinion, the only opinion that really counts. I urge you to seek Him for the more that He has available to you. But most of all I urge you to step into the place of your destiny... more fully conformed into the image of Jesus, the loving and disease destroying Savior....the kind, merciful and demon vanquishing Lord. You are an important part of His plan to change the world around you! The satisfaction of receiving healing and seeing hurting people dramatically touched by God awaits you!

Bibliography

Wimber, John. *Power Healing*, Harper San Francisco, 1987

Wimber, John. *Power Evangelism*, Regal, 1986

Johnson, Bill. *The Supernatural Power of a Transformed Mind*, Destiny Image, 2005

Johnson, Bill. *When Heaven Invades Earth*, destiny Image, 2003

Anderson, Dr. Neil T. *The Bondage Breaker, Victory Over The darkness*

Chapian, Marie. *Telling Yourself The Truth,* Bethany House, 2000

MacNutt, Francis. *The Healing Reawakening,* Chosen books, 2005

Blue, Ken, *Authority To Heal,* Intervarsity Press, Illinois 1987

Copies of this book can be ordered directly and at a discount.

And you can obtain info about orders or having a healing class or training for your group by emailing jpacilio@yahoo.com

Keep up with new testimonies and reports at jpacilio.wordpress.com